UT HISTORY: a timeline

1929-1934
GOLDEN AGE of HOLLYWOOD

ale characters of this period
often tough, sexually aggres-
, and independent, and they
engage in dalliances with
r women—all in movies the
eral public loved!

1930
NCY DREW *debuts*

ucky, level-headed teenager
cated to truth and justice.

1942
WARTIME

gs more than six million
en into the workforce in
yards, steel mills, foundries,
ehouses, offices, hospitals,
day care centers. "Rosie the
ter" is an icon of the born-
n—or situational—quirky-
e.

1950s
Time Warp

r World War II, social trends
rse: women exit the work-
e, people get married earli-
nd fertility rates are way
Other than in bohemian cap-
such as San Francisco and
York, quirkyalones go into
ng. According to Margaret
d, there are no unmarried
en in the 1950s. Heterosex-
tyranny reigns, and men as
as women are targeted.
helors are called immature,
ntile, narcissistic, deviant,
pathological.

1955
Rosa Parks

refuses to let a white bus rider
take her seat. Her act of defi-
ance sparks a 381-day boycott of
the Montgomery, Alabama, bus
system—and galvanizes the civil
rights movement: equal rights
and respect for all.

1960s
MARRIAGE MANIA

hits its peak: by 1962, over one-
third of all brides in the U.S. are
nineteen years old or younger.

1962
Helen Gurley Brown

busts out with *Sex and the Single
Girl*, a revolutionary advice book
that acknowledges unmarried
women enjoy sex.

1963
Betty Friedan's *The Feminine Mystique*

details the problem that has no
name (depressed housewives
with no sense of personal identity). Five million copies sell by
1970, laying the groundwork for
the modern feminist movement.

1960s and 1970s
CONSCIOUSNESS-RAISING

groups take root coast to coast.
Feminist critique of the nuclear
family eliminates some of the stigma attached to remaining single.

1969
STONEWALL RIOT

Official beginning of gay liberation movement—and a new era
of acceptance for nontraditional
sexual identities.

19
Free
You a

Marlo Thomas's
feely television show influences
budding quirkyalones with positive messages of self-acceptance.

1975
Laverne and Shirley

join cast of *Happy Days* (another
Boston-marriage-style arrangement).

1977
Three's Company

Jack, Janet, and Chrissy are a
'70s-style urban tribe.

JOANI BLANK OPENS *Good Vibrations*

which will become the nation's
premier clean well-lighted place
for sex toys.

1986

Notorious *Newsweek* article:
"SINGLE WOMEN OVER
40 HAVE LESS CHANCE TO
MARRY THAN TO BE
KILLED BY A TERRORIST."
Shock waves of anger, despair,
and disillusionment sweep the
country.

1980s-90s
Quirkytogether explosion

Strong, independent couples in
the limelight: Paul Newman and
Joanne Woodward; Susan
Sarandon and Tim Robbins; Kim
Gordon and Thurston Moore; etc.

1993
BESSIE + SADIE DELANEY

Two African-American women
who lived beyond the age of
100 and remained single the
whole time publish *Having
Our Say: The Delany Sisters'
First 100 Years*. In addition to
practicing yoga every morning
except Sunday, they jokingly
credit their single status as
the key to their longevity:
"We never had husbands
to worry us to death."

1998
Will and Grace and *Sex and the City* debut.

2000

GLORIA STEINEM WEDS at age 66.

FINLAND *elects*
single mother (and former radical) as the first woman president.

2003
NEWSWEEK publishes a
cover story on sexless marriages.
This time, single quirky-
alones can feel a little bit
smug.

2004
GROUNDBREAKING MANIFESTO

published. Quirkyalone consciousness continues to spread.

quirkyalone

quirkyalone

a manifesto for uncompromising romantics

Sasha Cagen

HarperSanFrancisco

A Division of HarperCollins*Publishers*

All credits appear on pages 158–159. Every effort has been made to trace the ownership of all copyrighted material included in this volume. Any errors that may have occurred are inadvertent and will be corrected in subsequent editions, provided notification is sent to the publisher.

HarperCollins books may be purchased for educational, business, or sales promotional use. For information please write: Special Markets Department, HarperCollins Publishers, Inc., 10 East 53rd Street, New York, NY 10022.

HarperCollins Web site: http://www.harpercollins.com
HarperCollins®, 📖®, and HarperSanFrancisco™ are trademarks of HarperCollins Publishers, Inc.

FIRST EDITION

Cover and book design by Laura Beers

Library of Congress Cataloging-in-Publication Data is available upon request.

ISBN 0–06–057898–X (cloth)
04 05 06 07 08 RRD(H) 10 9 8 7 6 5 4 3 2 1

quirkyalone (kwur.kee.uh.lohn) n. adj.

quirk•y *adj*. distinctive; unintentionally different; without artifice
a•lone *adj*. Apart from others, uncoupled; sometimes found in solitude
(enjoying it)

quirk•y•a•lone *n*. a person who enjoys being single (but is not opposed to
being in a relationship) and generally prefers to be alone rather than date for
the sake of being in a couple. With unique traits and an optimistic spirit; a
sensibility that transcends relationship status. Also *adj*. Of, relating to, or
embodying quirkyalones.
See also: romantic, idealist, independent.

Please note: A hyphen is neither desirable nor necessary when writing the
word "quirkyalone." Like the German word *zeitgeist* (*zeit* meaning time, and
geist meaning spirit), quirky and alone fuse together in a word that draws
upon its constituent parts to create a new meaning.

Quiz

ARE YOU A QUIRKYALONE?
(Or do you know someone who is?)
Examine the following statements and indicate
whether each one applies to you. You:

1. Display a talent for self-reflection.   T   F

2. Believe that life can be prosperous and
great with or without a mate.   T   F

3. Create and maintain chosen families of
friends.   T   F

4. Treat life as one big choose-your-own
adventure; there is no single road map for
adulthood.   T   F

5. Are not opposed to dating, but prefer not
to date for social convention.   T   F

6. Would rather be alone than be in a
relationship in which you have to hold back
an essential part of yourself.   T   F

7. Generally feel a sense of compulsion
to make a mark in culture and society,
to express yourself, whether through art,
writing, a small business, or activism.   T   F

8. Recognize the ways in which society
prescribes happiness primarily through
romantic love, and understand the failings
of such an approach.   T   F

9. Have had a taste or a glimpse of a great
love relationship (or encounter), which
intensifies your desire to remain open to the
possibility of finding a similar experience.   T   F

10. Possess a talent at deconstructing love
songs equal only to your vulnerability to them.   T   F

Determine your degree of quirkyaloneness.

**0 to 3 true answers: Sorry, you are not
quirkyalone.** But chances are good you may be
dating one, working with one, related to one, or
living with one and wanting to know that person
better. You also may be harboring closet
quirkyalone tendencies. Have you ever wondered
what it would be like to go to a movie alone?
Maybe you should try it.

4 to 6 true answers: Somewhat quirkyalone.
There are elements of the quirkyalone in almost
all of us: the iconoclast, the adventurer, the
romantic, the romantic obsessive. You embody
one-third to two-thirds of these qualities. You
probably need "a room of your own" while you
are in a relationship, but you manage to find
yourself, on a regular basis, in a coupled situation. Fascinating. If you are involved in a long-
term relationship, chances are good that you are
living a quirkytogether lifestyle. (Read more
about quirkytogethers in chapter 6.) Alternatively,
you may be someone who is completely comfortable being single and has no desire to find a
romantic relationship.

7 to 10 true answers: Very quirkyalone.
At long last. You have found your tribe, a brave
breed to resist the tyranny of coupledom in favor
of independent self-expression. Relatives may give
you quizzical looks, and so may co-workers, but
in your heart of hearts, you know that you are
following your inner voice. You may or may not
be participating in a conventional romance, but
always you are romancing the world. But you
have struggled on your own long enough. Now
there is a word for this mind-set, a way to put
our souls in communication with each other.
This book is for you, and the conversation is
just beginning. Welcome.

Emily Dickinson:
Quirky and alone, but not quirkyalone.
We are *sociable* people.

irkyalone

a response to the antiquirkyalone movement

chapter one
a girl and her word

"It's okay that I am alone."

"But maybe there is something wrong with me?"

"Maybe I'm just too picky."

"I'm young, I should be out there having sex."

"But I hate having sex with people I'm not really attracted to."

"Except when I'm traveling."

It was amazing how many times I could run through the same thoughts without arriving at any resolution.

I was not a social leper at age twenty-five. But I was not the most accomplished dater or girlfriend either.

Of course there had been flings, obsessions, dalliances, some of them even temporarily earth-moving, but none that had ever transformed me into someone's girlfriend for longer than four months. Being constitutionally incapable of halfhearted romantic involvement, I rarely played the dating game. Sometimes, while walking alone and getting lost in my thoughts, I felt strong and complete and good, at home with myself in my city and with my friends, but there were also moments when I would question my patterns and my confidence would ebb. Faced with some of my friends' steady relationships, I would wonder, What's the difference between them and me—or me and the consumers of *Modern*

Quirkyalone Thought to Ponder: "Uttering a word is like striking a note on the keyboard of the imagination."—Ludwig Wittgenstein

Bride magazine and *Cosmopolitan?* Why is it so much easier for them to find romantic partners? If there is a whole population of people who are running in and out of long-term relationships, how do they do it? And finally, the kicker, Am I the only one who feels this way? I might have convinced myself that I was, except for Tara, my soul mate during my first year of college. We spotted each other as kindred spirits during orientation and had been friends ever since. She matched me year for year in almost perpetual singledom.

Cut to New Year's Eve that year, 1998, almost 1999. In retrospect, it makes sense that quirkyalone was a New Year's baby. New Year's Eve at midnight—like the senior prom and the buddy system at camp—is one of those moments when we are all asked to line up two by two. It's also one of those turning-point holidays when we are asked to appraise our lives. That New Year's, I visited Tara for the holiday. We reminisced about our college-era zine, *Cupsize;* we dissected that wacky new show *Ally McBeal;* we checked in about the continued mystery of our singledom. The universal question seemed to be hanging in the air: Why was it always this way for us?

We'd lived long enough to start setting patterns. I was relating the last tragic story of my love life, she was relating the last tragic story of hers, ending with, Hmmm, didn't work out. What next? It was cathartic to recount another round of failed attempts at relationships and reveal the depths of our confusion, but we had no answers still. It felt like a rerun. How many times can you end a story with, "But it didn't work out"?

We had been talking since October about what we would do on New Year's Eve. We always had high hopes for such holidays even though we knew most New Year's Eves turned out awful or, more to the point, spectacularly awful, with us freezing to death in the streets of Manhattan. This year we decided we would take a new, more adult approach. Instead of trying to find the Shangri-La of New Year's parties in Manhattan, with an unending vista of unattached, charming New Yorkers dying to meet us, we would take a safer approach. We would wed ourselves to our friend Marissa's party in Brooklyn and lay down some roots. After a lifetime of New Year's searching, we were ready to make it one party, all night long.

I still expected to find a midnight kiss. How hard could it be? Stunningly, after my third reconnaissance mission around the apartment and on the roof, by 11PM I was forced to make a negative assessment. Things were not looking good. Many friendly familiar faces, but no mysterious strangers. At this point, all I had left was hope for a wild card, a late arrival. My only prospect was the mysterious, as yet unseen unarrival. Even at 11:45, my eyes were trained on the door. I'm not a quitter, and if there was any chance of a midnight kiss, I was going to find it.

As we began the countdown to 1999, I called a halt to the search, and my vision broadened to take in the whole room. Looking around the room, I saw something I hadn't seen before. I realized what I was looking at. A sea of people not kissing. In all my obsessive searching, I had never considered this possibility: a New Year's Eve Party Totally Devoid of Midnight Kiss. I like to think of that as the click, when I moved from thinking that Tara and I were the only ones to seeing us as part of a group, a moment, and perhaps even a movement.

The morning after, Tara, Marissa, and I met at a diner for our 'M ere. traditional New Year's Day brunch. We talked resolutions, of course, and again tried to figure out why we had just witnessed a whole party of people not kissing at midnight. After polishing off our coffee, pierogies, French toast, and home fries, we bundled up to walk to the ATM. That's when and where it

——— A L O N E

goofyalone

bizarrealone

peculiaralone

crazyalone

wackyalone

nuttyalone

freakyalone

strangealone

eccentricalone

oddalone

idiosyncraticalone

zanyalone

offbeatalone

anomalousalone

kookyalone

Clearly,

it had to be

quirkyalone.

"We're all pretty bizarre. Some of us are just better at hiding it."
—"Andrew Clark" (Emilio Estevez)

The fine line between "quirky" and "socially deviant" behavior: When "Allison" (Ally Sheedy) used dandruff to make her pencil drawing come alive with snow, we all celebrated our own inner weirdo, but wondered if she had crossed over into "gross."

The Breakfast Club, the classic '80s flick from John Hughes, gave us the familiar archetypes of criminal, athlete, princess, basket case, and brain. In the end, the film proved that there is more than a little quirkiness in all of us.

happened: in an ATM vestibule on a brutally cold, windy New Year's Day. I punched in my code. While waiting for the money to spit out, I turned around to them with a spontaneous declaration: "You know who we are? We're the quirkyalones!"

There was no theory. There was no definition. But I could see that Marissa and Tara understood. They smiled with an instant recognition. Of course we were single; we were a gang of cool, adventurous, distinctively attractive women leading often-improvisational lives. To put this state of being into a single word gave new life to our conversation. It also provided a point of reference, a word that, later on, others were able to use as a tool to communicate and organize themselves.

why Quirky?
why Alone?

For some people, this jumble of syllables immediately rings with meaning, and all the right adjectives come to mind: *independent, yearning, perfectionist, solid, romantic.* Others want to know "why quirky?" and "why alone?" The easy answer is that I never deliberated alternative words. The word *quirkyalone* came to me in a flash, fully formed, that morning with my friends at the ATM. I can't imagine how any other words would connote the same meaning. But for all those who don't intuitively understand these word choices, let's look a little closer at their meanings.

"For me, quirky is the courage to be yourself whether it's popular or not. There's a vulnerability and yet a strength." —Jeni, quirkytogethe

Merriam-Webster defines *quirk* as "an abrupt twist or curve" and "a peculiar trait: idiosyncrasy." In a sense, quirkyness is inherent to all of us: we are all individuals, so we are all quirky. And yet it is generally acknowledged that there are quirky people and not-so-quirky people. What is the difference? Perhaps truly quirky people are the ones who don't have the option of camouflaging their individuality: they're just uncontrollably themselves.

Quirky is human. It's real. It's unintentional difference, being distinctive without artifice. Quirky is the cowlick in your hair that won't lie flat; the nail polish that remains chipped (especially the chipped nail polish on a finger pressing a button in the elevator of a corporate office tower). A mother writing her daughter an e-mail with the subject line "Soap" while the e-mail mentions nothing even remotely pertaining to soap is quirky; so is going on a road trip to see the great diners of America or eating yogurt and cottage cheese with every meal.

Making "Unconventional Iconoclast" your personal ad headline is *not* quirky. Quirky people know better than to advertise this quality; they have more creative ways of showing that they are a little "different." Be a little too bald about your quirkyness, and you may be perceived as a pseudoquirky, one who tries to cultivate an air of difference for a charm factor. Quirky also is not going to a gym class and doing completely different exercises from the rest of the class. You're marching to the beat of your own drum, but why? Why even come to the class? You're annoying all the other people by flailing your arms in conflicting patterns. Quirky is about being yourself, but it's not aggressive and it should not harm others.

There are other meanings: *Quirky* means taking an experimental approach to adulthood, not always following an automatic path. It's appreciating the benefits of alienation: realizing that living off the predefined grid can be freeing and fruitful. A certain introversion may be inherent: you have the ability to amuse yourself, to set your own code of behavior and live in your own world.

"There seems to be an element of acceptance to the word *quirky*. It's not something you're trying to change."
—Sarah, quirkyalone

"THE LIMITS OF MY LANGUAGE ARE THE LIMITS OF MY MIND. ALL I KNOW IS WHAT I HAVE WORDS FOR."—LUDWIG WITTGENSTEIN

Some people ask whether using the word *quirky* as opposed to *odd* is a public relations move because we don't want to be thought of as strange. While it's true that calling someone kooky or weird is usually a put-down, the word *quirky* describes something distinct. *Quirky* is softer than *odd*; it's somehow endearing, even lovable. We can be annoyed by people's quirks, but we can also develop a fondness for them. Witness the extremely frequent use of the word in the descriptions of romantic comedies, in which quirky people (against all odds) find each other: *"Punch-Drunk Love* is a sweet, surreal, and quirky love story that will make your heart dance." The *wackyalone* or *oddalone,* I think we can all agree, probably would not have the same resonance.

What about *alone?* What's the connection? *Alone* can strike some people as a misnomer, as too final and damning. The meaning of *alone* should be understood not as "lonely," "solitary," or "desolate," but as a declaration of independence, a willingness to step out from the crowd to follow one's own instincts. It's more in line with *Merriam-Webster*'s fourth definition: "incomparable, unique." It also stands for single. Putting *quirky* together with *alone* implies the ability to enjoy one's aloneness, whether one is single or not.

The Japanese Quirkyalone: Wagamana
Quirkyalone may be primarily a first-world development and of its adherent citizens, in countries where large numbers of women and men can be economically independent. But it's not only an American thing. In Japan, more than half of women are still single at thirty, compared with 37 percent in the United States. According to Peggy Orenstein's report for the *New York Times Magazine,* some Japanese single women have begun to embrace the word *wagamama,* meaning "selfish" or "willful," as an ironic badge of honor. According to Orenstein, the word is being transformed to mean something closer to "choosy" or even "self-determining." Women's magazines have caught the trend, featuring headlines like "Restaurants for the Wagamama You."

"but you don't look quirky"

What does the Quirkyalone Nation look like? Can you tell if someone is quirkyalone just by looking at them? The complicated relationship between outer garments and inner state came to a head for me one night at a party of media types in San Francisco. Two new acquaintances couldn't believe that I was the person behind this idea: "But you don't look quirky!" they cried. So what if I wear jeans from a well-known, San Francisco–based conglomerate? Do I need to be the tattooed-pierced-cat-eyed-glasses person in a polka dot dress in order to be a (female) quirkyalone?

The weeks following found me meditating on the outward appearance of quirkyness. I wondered whether such a thing is possible and if I should I stop tweezing my eyebrows to achieve harmony between my public image and my inner spirit (to look quirky in a Frida Kahlo sort of way). Bah, I decided. Quirky is as quirky does. Plus, I don't want to go back to those unibrow days.

The bottom line is: quirky is something we are, not something we wear. Quirkyalones can be preppy or hip, bike messengers or country-western singers. A quirkyalone may wear a Nancy Reaganesque red blazer and gold earrings. Another may don a dazzling pink dress constructed almost exclusively of feathers. The rule of thumb is to be yourself. Kindred spirits don't always shop at the same stores or listen to the same music; quirkyness, by definition, involves an element of surprise.

Which one is quirkyalone?

You can't tell. Quirky is something we are, not something we wear.

Q & A on QAs

Q. Can the quirkyalone be a man?

A. Yes, yes, yes! quirkyalone is a mind-set and a way of life: anyone can be a quirkyalone. It's worth pointing out, however, that our culture is already rife with archetypes for male loners: Odysseus, Western cowboy, geek, James Dean, solitary indie-rock boy, and so forth. The scant few labels that describe a woman alone are pejorative: *spinster* and *old maid*. For this reason we often use the feminine pronoun for quirkyalone in this book to create a positive alternative for women. It's part of our diligent campaign to battle a thousands-year-old history of oppressing single women. See "Attention Men: You Are Not Forgotten!" on page 9 for more.

Q. If I am a quirkyalone, does this mean I have to be celibate?

A. Not unless you choose to be.

Q. Does this fundamental quality preclude me from meeting "the one"? Will I be so choosy that I will always be alone?

A. Vexing, for sure. Many of us obsess on this very question. Don't despair. Despairing never helps. Being quirkyalone may, in fact, help you in the search for love. You won't waste years in mediocre relationships, and the training you receive alone is valuable no matter what course your life takes. As many self-help authors note, being comfortable alone is a crucial foundation for intimacy with another person.

Q. What if I am quirkyalone until I find a partner and then find myself reenacting every sick cliché I once railed against?

A. For starters, know that you are not alone. The quirkyalone's deeply romantic nature can cause those who do fall in love to fall hard, sometimes even leading to obsessive behavior. Read more about the perils of QA love on page 55, "The

Dark Side of the Quirkyalone: Romantic Obsession (R.O.)." But you don't have to be a cliché. Recognizing ways that your new couple status contradicts your aforementioned belief system is the start of being quirkytogether, a more liberated version of coupling that will allow you to preserve the best parts of being single and coupled. Read more on the transition to quirkytogether in chapter 6.

Q. Are quirkyalones able to marry?
A. Yes, heterosexual quirkyalones can marry. The same-sex unions of gay quirkyalones are still being discriminated against.

Q. I know someone who is constantly hooking up but doesn't get into relationships. Is she quirkyalone?
A. Good question. If your friend's standards for companionship are very high, but for a Saturday night fling very low, she goes by another name. This person is a quirkyslut. She should wear that title proudly. (Read more about quirkysluts on page 62).

ATTENTION MEN! YOU ARE NOT FORGOTTEN.

Men often ask whether they too can be quirkyalones. The answer has always been yes, with the caveat that we often use the feminine pronoun as a sort of affirmative action for single women. Some men feel a bit annoyed by this; they feel marginalized by the quirkyalone movement's images of vibrators, discussions of spinsters, and celebration of other feminine cultural paraphernalia. Men from this subset send in protest letters. Mark writes, "C'mon! You need a quirkyalone male category too. The male versions ('loner,' etc.) are up there with the female 'spinster.' I'm not out to shoot up a McDonald's ('angry young man')."

While it's true that there are stereotypes for single men (the Peter Pan, the mama's boy, the commitmentphobe, the nerd, the Casanova), the point is that quirkyalone men don't need to be shortchanged with their own category and turned into second-class quirkyalones: the essential emotional experience is the same. Chris, a musician in his late thirties, recalls his first experience of adolescent pressure regarding his relationship status. His father called from out of state and asked his mother, "Does he have a girlfriend?" His mother answered, "No, I don't think so." His father said, "Well, that's not too normal, is it?" Chris was only fourteen at the time.

But let's face it: while quirkyalone men face some level of stigma, the oppression that quirkyalone women have faced has been more severe. A woman who holds out is more likely to be branded "picky, picky, picky" in much of the country. There's a reason that when it comes to pop culture Americans fixate on single women as opposed to single men—for a woman to remain unmarried is much more threatening to mainstream ideals about what it means to be a woman. So while the voices and experiences of men are definitely included in this book (we love our sensitive quirkyalone men and all the insights they have to share), our brothers are asked to understand why—at this stage of the revolution—there will be more emphasis on the female experience. There will be pictures of vibrators. Prepare yourself.

Tom Hadjuk, an English teacher from Seattle, understands quirkyalone's particular relevance to women: "Quirkyalone finally put into words what we most need in relationships—the confidence to be ourselves and to let others be themselves. The quirkyalone is clearly a feminist idea, and a vital one. Although men are supposedly the ones who desire solitude, many men aim to redefine women through relationships. Too often the women compromise, the men don't, and we have ourselves a disaster. Male quirkyalones may have enjoyed a more secure place in society, but female quirkyalones have faced some monumental pressure. Well, the time has come. The quirkyalones are rising. And not everything that rises converges."

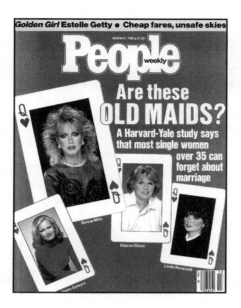

WHY WE USE THE FEMININE PRONOUN FOR
THE WORD *QUIRKYALONE*:
WE MUST CONCENTRATE NOW ON THOSE
WHO NEED HELP MOST.

Name: Jerry Wayne White Jr.

Age: 27

Hometown: Rochester, Mich.

Current town: Rochester, Mich. (amazingly enough)

Job: Student

Length of time quirkyalone: I've always been quirky something—usually alone, a couple times together.

Favorite quirkyalone activities: Reading for free at Barnes & Noble in comfy chairs, Borders, too, but not so much, shooting and editing video, playing guitar and singing, writing, sleeping, planning

Personal QA motto: We embrace this label because it validates our otherness—at once celebrating solitude while making us feel not so alone or bad about it.

MEET THE QUIRKYALONES

Name: Klover Kim

Age: 26

Hometown: Nascarlot, N.C.

Current town: San Francisco, Calif.

Relationship status: In my first relationship

Favorite Golden Girl: Sophia, tough outside, softie inside; takes no snuff, caustic with age, and always carries a big bag

Personal QA motto: Solitude, in solidarity!

Name: Niecie Noflaws (nickname)

Age: 44

Hometown: San Francisco, Calif.

Current town: San Francisco, Calif.

Job: Personal and Style Assistant

Length of time quirkyalone: Ever since I can remember

Favorite Golden Girl: I like them all, just like if I had to pick my favorite *Sex and the City* girl. But if I had to choose, I like Sophia, and Bea too!

Favorite quirkyalone activities: I like doing my arts and crafts! I love any kind of "snorkeling" (my word for shopping). I prefer to do it alone, but have been known to make it a social activity (w/ one person). Bookstores are a place where you can find me, especially if there's a café area! I like to travel alone.

Personal QA motto: Not that I need to cheer myself on, but since age thirty-six, I have come up with rhymes that grow with my current age. It's like being quirkyalone, you have to fight the standards of youth in America: "thirty-seven and now I'm in heaven," "thirty-eight and feeling great," "thirty-nine-and-feeling-oh-so-fine-and-divine," and "hot, sultry, and forty." Now I'm on "forty-four and ready for more."

Name: Amber Mottram

Age: 24

Hometown: Lakeland, Fla.

Current town: Jacksonville, Fla.

Job: Grad student/receptionist

Length of time quirkyalone: At least two years

Favorite quirkyalone activities: Drawing, video games, driving aimlessly

Personal QA motto: It's so much more exciting to move to a new city, start a job, etc. with the possibility of "I might meet someone."

The Quirkyalone

Loners are the last true romantics

I am, perhaps, what you might call deeply single. Almost never ever in a relationship. Until recently, I wondered whether there might be something weird about me. But then lonely romantics began to grace the covers of *TV Guide* and *Mademoiselle*. From *Ally McBeal* to *Sex and the City,* a spotlight came to shine on the forever single. If these shows had touched such a nerve in our culture, I began to think, perhaps I was not so alone after all. The morning after New Year's Eve (another kissless one, of course), a certain jumble of syllables came to me. When I told my friends about my idea, their faces lit up with instant recognition: the quirkyalone.

If Jung was right, that people are different in fundamental ways that drive them from within, then the quirkyalone is simply to be added to the pantheon of personality types collected over the 20th century. Only now, when the idea of marrying at age 20 has become thoroughly passé, are we quirkyalones emerging in greater numbers.

We are the puzzle pieces who seldom fit with other puzzle pieces. Romantics, idealists, eccentrics, we inhabit single-dom as our natural resting state. In a world where proms and marriage define the social order, we are, by force of our personalities and inner strength, rebels.

For the quirkyalone, there is no patience for dating just for the sake of not being alone. We want a miracle. Out of millions, we have to find the one who will understand.

Better to be untethered and open to possibility: living for the exhilaration of meeting someone new, of

By Sasha Cagen

To-Do List

not knowing what the night will bring. We qui alones seek momentous meetings.

By the same token, being alone is understood wellspring of feeling and experience. There is a bit sweet fondness for silence. All those nights alon they bring insight.

Sometimes, though, we wonder whether we h painted ourselves into a corner. Standards that sta out high only become higher once you realize the c tours of this existence. When we do fir match, we verge on obsessive—or we res

And so, a community of like-minded s is essential. Since fellow quirkyalones are not ab dant (we are probably less than 5 percent of the p ulation), I recommend reading the patron sain solitude: German poet Rainer Maria Rilke. Even years after its publication, *Letters to a Young Poet* feels like it was written for us: "You should not yourself be confused in your solitude by the fact there is something in you that wants to break ou it," Rilke writes. "People have (with the help of c ventions) oriented all their solutions toward the and toward the easiest side of easy, but it is clear we must hold to that which is difficult."

Rilke is right. Being quirkyalone can be diffic Everyone else is part of a couple! Still, there advantages. No one can take our lives away by bre ing up with us. Instead of sacrificing our social c stellation for the one all-consuming individual, seek empathy from friends. We have significant *oth*

And so, when my friend asks me whether be quirkyalone is a life sentence, I say, yes, at the core, is always quirkyalone. But when one quirkyalone fi another, oooh la la. The earth quakes.

From To-Do List *(premiere issue).*

chapter two

birth of a movement

A month after returning to San Francisco from that holiday trip back east, I wrote a rough definition of this new word. I e-mailed the initial draft to my friend Ali for a little feedback. Ali didn't tell me, but that night she forwarded the e-mail to her friends; they continued to do the same. By Friday my e-mail account had exceeded its limit, and the inbox was filled with mysterious notes from strangers: "Thank you, I thought I was the only one on the planet who felt this way."

The essay eventually appeared in print almost a year later in the first issue of my independent magazine, *To-Do List*. I expected that the idea might make a small splash in San Francisco, my adopted hometown. To my surprise, the editors of *Utne Reader* (circulation 230,000) e-mailed to request permission to reprint the piece in its September 2000 issue. From here on, we were in uncharted territory. For months following, hundreds of letters, postcards, poetry from prisoners (complete with marriage proposals), suggestions of more quirkyalones throughout history, and mix tapes arrived in response. They all said the same thing: that this definition validated a condition they had never seen pinpointed before. I often sat on the sidewalk outside the post office reading these letters, slack-jawed in amazement. Every day there was a new note from some unlikely person, not at all who I had expected to fit the quirkyalone demographic (single women in their twenties — me, basically).

Veronica, a teacher from New York, wrote, "One of the ironies that you didn't point out in your article is that we quirkyalones are often quite accomplished, attractive women. It's not like we're homely Jane Eyre types! I am a cheerful extrovert who goes to parties, runs a book club, often goes dancing with friends, etc. I travel in the U.S. and abroad, and I have friends everywhere of all colors, orientations, and descriptions (I'm an African American woman in my midthirties). I say all this because there are times when I too scratch my head and wonder the same thing that this woman from an auto detailing shop once asked me, apropos of nothing: 'Why hasn't someone come along and plucked you off the shelf by now?' I was aghast, but then again, it wasn't the first time someone asked me that."

Jeff in Kentucky shared, "I'm not a big believer in labels, but this one definitely struck a nerve with me. In breaking off our relationship, my most recent girlfriend tried to play matchmaker. I explained to her that I was alone when she came along and was content to be alone again. It was a struggle trying to make her understand how I felt."

Soon after, reporters started to call, treating me as if I were some kind of pundit on singledom. The word spread through digital word of mouth, the independent media, and finally the mainstream media. Stories about quirkyalone were translated into Czech and Chinese. The essay spawned three online communities, one of which is still active, and a new holiday, International Quirkyalone Day. Two years later a friend called and left an excited message: "Did you see the guide for the San Francisco Independent Film Festival? This woman has organized a film series of short films called 'Fuel for the Quirkyalone'!"

September 1, 2000: 0

November 25, 2000: 51

September 13, 2003: 800

Hits generated by the word *quirkyalone* on Google as of:

Google

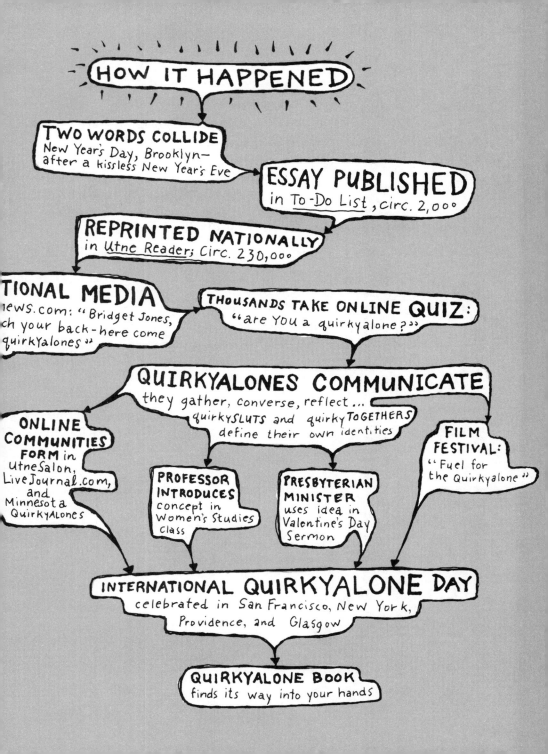

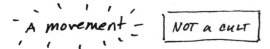

quirkyalone

— A movement — | NOT a cult |

To tell you the truth, it was strange to watch a word that had previously lived only in my diary get splashed all over the Internet. As time passed, it became obvious that *quirkyalone* had struck a chord, and the wave of attention that resulted was big—and growing.

QUIRKYALONES UNITE

Words are always a reflection of the culture from which they spring, and every word is first a neologism, humanmade. *Quirkyalone* arrived at a moment when many others found the available system of classification lacking. In 2000, *Time* magazine declared that we are in the midst of a "major societal shift" as "single women, once treated as virtual outcasts, have moved to the center of our social and cultural life." Soon after, *The Economist* reported that the "people who now dominate and shape the rich world's city life, not just in New York and London, but increasingly in Tokyo, Stockholm, Paris and Santiago [are] well-educated, single professionals in their 20s and 30s."

Surprising to me then, but not in retrospect, was that responses to this wee manifesto flooded in from all directions. The time was right for a new idea. Biologist Richard Dawkins has a name for an idea that spreads through soci-

Name: Jamie Giedinghagen
Age: 26
Hometown: St. Louis, Mo.
Current town: Washington, D.C.
Job: Website Administrator/Project Manager for the International Centre for Missing and Exploited Children
Length of time quirkyalone: Always. I just didn't know there was a name for it.
Relationship status: Single
Personal QA motto: Quirkyalone is about being my own best friend. Please see Whitney Houston's "The Greatest Love of All"!
Note: Jamie is the founder of the quirkyalone LiveJournal.com forum.

ety: a *meme*. Dawkins defines the meme as a "unit of cultural transmission" and says that memes are "tunes, ideas, catch-phrases, clothes fashions, ways of making pots or building arches. . . ." Dawkins relates a meme's survival rate in culture to its psychological appeal. If an idea truly captures the imagination, answering a psychological question or puzzle, it spreads from "brain to brain."

Quirkyalone is not an illness. But first hearing about it is akin to getting a diagnosis. Often when you find there is an explanation for how you feel (or at least a word that encapsulates it and confirms that others grapple with the same thing), the fears diminish and the pain goes away.

When we talk about a quirkyalone movement, then, we mean a group of people who see themselves as part of a community, in conversation with each other, helping to fend off the toxic ideas that are propagated by the mainstream media. The quirkyalone movement is not headquartered in Washington, D.C.; there probably will be no Quirkyalone March on Washington. (Although there is an American Association of Single People, believe it or not.) But there are core values. Quirkyalone stands in opposition to saccharine, archaic notions of romantic love. It stands for self-respect, independent spirit, creativity, true love, and confidence. Maralyn Lois Palak, a reader from Pennsylvania, predicted a movement when she read the original manifesto. She wrote, "I can't remember when I related to an article so completely as I did to yours. . . . I think your article is more than an article. It celebrates a zanily free human condition so often pathologized by the media and others. I think there is a movement here."

Quirkyalone Critics

Not everyone in the media understands us, but that's okay. Quirkyalones don't *want* to be understood by everyone.

"*Quirky* connotes flaky, not responsible; someone with low self-esteem. *Alone* represents depressed, overly independent, and unmatchable."
—Hollywood matchmaking guru Wendee Mason in an interview with Fox News

"I'm all for figuring out your own shit outside the context of a relationship, but there's some stuff you can only figure out with someone else. . . . Unfortunately, for the quirkyalone, the longer you wait, the harder it becomes. And then you end up in situations . . . where dinner with someone becomes a life crisis."
—Josey Vogels, "Alone Again Naturally," mymessybedroom.com

"I proselytize about quirkyalone a lot. I'm not just interested in figuring it out for myself. I need to spread it." —Margaret Fenner, **33**

In a sense, the quirkyalone community is what the anthropologist Victor Turner defines as *communitas*, a collection of liminal people who live outside fixed categories and classifications, whose conversations are a "kind of institutional capsule or pocket which contains the germ of future social developments, or social change." Out of that community comes a new social category beyond single, coupled, married, or divorced. In the future, when you check *quirkyalone* on your W-2 form, you will be indicating that you are able to live a full and happy life whether you are coupled up or not.

Let's be clear about one thing. The quirkyalone movement is not a cult. You do not have to go door to door to recruit new members (unless you want to) or cut ties with non-quirkyalones. You don't even have to be single to belong. On the one hand, quirkyalone is a celebration of our emancipation from compulsory coupledom; on the other hand, it's an antidote to the silicone version of love presented in reality-dating shows and network television.

There is of course a certain irony in individuated, quirky women and men flocking together under the banner of a label. Quirky people are often highly distinctive and idiosyncratic, people who resist categorization. But who wants to be alone all the time? As American Express never tires of telling us, membership does have its benefits. We may be strong as individuals, but there are limits to the changes that any one individual can make. Whenever you are doing something that goes against the grain, you need the support of others.

"I really liked the idea of quirkyalone. It gives a name to what kind of person I am. A lot of girls who are quirkyalone might get stuck with the label *spinster* or *old maid*. *Quirkyalone* implies a sort of hipness, a reverence for being alone and choosy. It's something that you want to be identified with." — Sarah Hamilton, a student in Fort Collins, Colo.

QUIRKYALONE NATION

Who are we, and why are we here? Seeking answers to these fundamental questions, the researchers at QAHQ (Sasha and professional QA Reyhan H.) sent out an e-mail survey to *To-Do List* subscribers and others who sent e-mails in response to the original manifesto. We also posted the questionnaire on online bulletin boards. The information below combines the raw data collected through this survey with interpretation from the experts—ourselves. Of course, you should bear in mind that these are just the self-diagnosed, and there may be a lot of older and rural quirkyalones who are not on the Internet and haven't heard about the movement yet. Which is another way of saying, until the U.S. Census Bureau recognizes us, any profile will be incomplete.

OCCUPATION

Clearly quirkyalones are creative types. Their occupations are infinitely varied, but one thing is true of them as a group. They often distinguish between "what I do for a living" and "who I really am." Whether their extracurricular activity takes the form of surfing, knitting, writing, saving the world through activism, or making art out of dryer lint, these passions can take on as much importance as "the job" or "the relationship." The darker side: career or an artistic vision can become overly consuming, taking on an unduly large portion of a quirkyalone's life. A sample of their professions and dream jobs, according to our survey.

profession:

unemployed video store clerk
programmer
sales manager
sign language interpreter
freelance copywriter
stripper
office manager
labor organizer
lobbyist
library assistant
policy analyst

don't want to talk about it

dream job:

writer/filmmaker
more senior programmer
director of protocol for a vacation resort
herbalist
singer in Broadway show
art student
travel writer
collective farmer
writer
women's health and sexuality educator
to be free...no office job, living in cabin
    with organic garden
professional friend

SEXUAL ORIENTATION

83% heterosexual
(includes metrosexual(*))
11% gay/lesbian
5% bisexual
1% anything that moves

A gay-friendly, open-minded population.

Estimates put the percentage of gay people at between 7 to 10 percent of the U.S. population. The percentage in the QA world is almost double. Why? Obviously the similarities between being gay and being quirkyalone go beyond feeling a little alienated at large family gatherings. Part of our bond can be explained by the fact that the ideal of lifelong monogamy through a state-sanctioned marriage is not available to most gay people; by default, gay men and lesbians create their own structures for relationships, not unlike the quirkytogether. Another key similarity is the acceptance and embrace of friendship as a primary relationship. In response to homophobia, gay people have always turned to friends as family. Bi-curiosity may also be endemic to the QA worldview, especially in college-age quirkyalones who are investigating their sexual identities. If you're looking for that one-in-a-million miracle, why limit the search to fifty percent of the population?

*metrosexual: the urban phenomenon of straight men who look and act gay, i.e. excellent grooming skills and good taste in home decor.

GEOGRAPHY

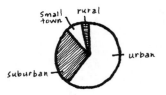

60% urban
30% suburban
7% small town
3% rural

Primarily an urban phenomenon, but not entirely.

Quirkyalone is primarily an urban phenomenon. Urban quirkyalones court and fall in love with cities, similar to the way that people fall in love with other human beings. Quirkyalones often flock to havens for nonconformists, such as San Francisco, New York, Portland, and Austin. Many others reside in major cities such as Chicago, Atlanta, Boston, Los Angeles, and Minneapolis. The metaphor of city-as-lover is common among many. It's not unheard of for some QAs to throw urban anniversary parties (for example, a party to celebrate ten years in Portland). But quirkyalones also reside in suburbia, small towns, and rural areas. Paul Walker wrote in after hearing about quirkyalone on NPR: "The straight male 'loner' is slightly more accepted than your typical female 'quirkyalone,' but we have more in common than you might think. Just try being one in Iowa."

AGE

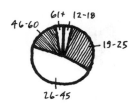

- 61+
- 12-18
- 46-60
- 19-25
- 26-45

12-18: 3%
19-25: 29%
26-45: 47%
46-60: 18%
61+: 3%

No, it's not just a phase.

The greatest number of responses to our surveys came from people in the 26-to-45 category, and many of those were in their late twenties and early thirties. Not surprising, since the late twenties are when all those wedding invitations start clogging our mailboxes, and we start to seriously assess how our attitudes compare to the generally received wisdom about relationships. As explained in chapter 3, however, people come to terms with quirkyalone status at ages ranging from 13 to 59, and for most of us, once we do, it's a lifelong orientation. As our ranks grow, so will our age diversity. The good news: By the time GenXers reach retirement age, the percentage of quirky-elders will no doubt have increased. Currently quirkyalones number about 5 percent of the U.S. population, and the numbers are sure to grow.

Don't belive the hype about growing old alone!
Retirement is going to be fun. The revolution will continue in the games room.

"For me, the late twenties were the hardest. I started to realize it was quite possible that I could spend the rest of my life alone, and I internalized all my inability to be in a stable relationship to the point that I thought there was something entirely wrong with me. I was starting to crawl through some transition, but the road was really narrow and I couldn't see anything around me. I knew that I had to recreate the conception of my life or else I was going to be really depressed and disappointed that I failed at something that seemed to be a birthright. That birthright [of being in a couple] was supposed to be given to you at some point in your twenties, and in my late twenties I was most anxious because I saw it slipping away. Was anyone else in my life going through this? Yes. My friend, who I thought was a totally cool person, independent. Seeing her depression and anxiety made me think, This is really pathetic. She spent so much time thinking about being single and going to dating services and self-improvement and codependent anonymous meetings and going on diets—everything was focused on the 'other.' I felt like she was killing herself in the process of trying to merge with someone else. Her obsession jolted me out of mine." —Kara Herold

Name:
Anne Maria Hardeman

Age: Over 35, 37, 39, 41—is
the pattern clear now? I'm
so over my age and never
judge my interactions with
folks based on it.

Hometown: San José, Calif.

Current town: Oakland, Calif.

Job: Artist

Relationship status: Single

Favorite Golden Girls: My
mother and her friends.
Their energy and social life
remind me to call my friends,
see my friends, and stay on
track with my life goals.

Personal QA motto: You can
have a road trip experience
at home.

GENDER

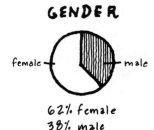

62% female
38% male

Yes, men can be quirkyalone
too. It's just more rare.

If your first thought when you heard the
word "quirkyalone" was that it described
a single girl in the city, you're not far off;
more than half of us do fit that profile. But
like any cliché, the single-girl-in-the-city
image just scratches the surface. Both
men and women identify as quirkyalone.
However, the female cohort is stronger.

PETS

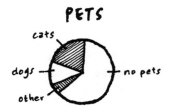

67% have no pets
33% have pets, of those:
  20% cats
  10% dogs
  3% other *

Only a third of quirkyalones have
pets. Were you surprised?

*including parakeets, goldfish and iguanas

Warning:
the antiquirkyalone movement

WARNING: THESE BOOKS MAY BE HAZARDOUS TO YOUR HEALTH

As the quirkyalone movement grows and takes hold around the world, celebrating the values of sincerity, individuality, authenticity, being yourself from the first date on—and discovering who you are instead of placing all emphasis on being in a couple—we must also remember that we are still living with a well-financed, highly organized, and powerful *antiquirkyalone* movement. This movement is also known as the status quo, or popular culture. Its glossy magazines celebrate young celebrity couples with photos of their extravagantly lavish weddings (unions that often dissolve soon after the magazine reaches newsstands). It promotes Botox to smooth away wrinkles—and take away your ability to frown and express emotion, to be human and real (quirky!). This sect, which usually targets women, also publishes an arsenal of literature and pamphlets to promote a strict timetable for marriage and to devalue goals other than finding a spouse. Unfortunately, our enemies have a strong hold in the publishing industry; they put out virtually the same book year after year. We in the quirkyalone movement are doing our best to counter these insidious messages, but we want to caution you about their prevalence. Following is just a small sample of the titles they may use to undermine your confidence.

If you see these "books" carried in your local chain bookstore, please do not be alarmed. *How to Marry the Man of Your Choice* (1984); *Smart Women, Foolish Choices* (1985); *How to Find Another Husband: By Someone Who Did* (1985); *Husband Hunting: How to Win at the Mating Game* (1986); *Why Isn't My Daughter Married? Daughters Tell Mothers the Real Reason They're Single* (1988); *The Best Places to Meet Good Men* (1991); *What Men Really Want* (1991); *The Secrets of Winning Men* (1993); *Getting to "I Do"* (1994); *The Rules: Time-Tested Secrets for Capturing the Heart of Mr. Right* (1995); *Desirable Men: How to Find Them* (1997); *The Real Rules: How to Find the Right Man for the Real You* (1997); *The Rules II: More Rules to Live and Love By* (1997); *What Men Want: Three Professional Single Men Reveal What It Takes to Make a Man Yours* (1998); *The Surrendered Wife: A Practical Guide to Finding Intimacy, Peace, and Passion with Your Man* (2001); *The Surrendered Single: A Practical Guide to Attracting and Marrying the Man Who's Right for You* (2002); *Why There Are No Good Men Left: The Romantic Plight of the New Single Woman* (2002).

Sasha Cagen's To-Do List
creates community

By Craig Marine
OF THE EXAMINER STAFF

S ASHA CAGEN, being bright, lit-
erate and publisher of an intelligent, witty and ambitious new
magazine, knows irony when it
slaps her in the mug. She

San Francisco Chronicle

WEEKEND PREVIEW

FRIDAY, FEBRUARY 14, 2003

'Quirky' Day offers singular alternative to Valentine's

By Dave Ford
CHRONICLE STAFF WRITER

Sasha Cagen laughs a lot as
she talks about Valentine's
Day.

After all, you're never alone
when you're with others who are
quirkyalones.

Especially when they, like you,
are quirkyalones. ...
That's right: quirkyalones.
... International Quirkyalone
... something

BIRTH OF A MOVEMENT · BIRTH OF A MOVEMENT · BIRTH OF A MOVEMENT · FAM

Hello my name is Amy

I am
- ☐ Quirkyalone
- ☒ Quirkytogether
- ☐ Quirkyslut
- ☐ in support of Quirkyalones

I believe in
- ☐ God
- ☐ Martinis
- ☒ Living free and wild

I like to hold the hands of
- ☐ You
- ☐ Grandmothers
- ☒ Babies
- ☐ Aliens
- ☐ No one
If I were on a reality T

Behind my mask I am
- ☐ warm and fuzzy
- ☐ ice clear
- ☐ on

Hello my name is NICK

I am
- ☒ Quirkyalone
- ☐ Quirkytogether
- ☐ Quirkyslut
- ☐ in support of Quirkyalones

I believe in
- ☐ God
- ☒ Martinis
- ☐ Living free and wild

I like to hold the hands of
- ☒ You
- ☐ Grandmothers
- ☐ Babies
- ☐ Aliens
- ☐ No one
If I were

Behind my mask I am
- ☐ warm and fuzzy
- ☐ the midd

Hello my name is Carrie

I am
- ☒ Quirkyalone
- ☐ Quirkytogether
- ☐ Quirkyslut
- ☐ in support of Quirkyalones

I believe in
- ☐ God
- ☐ Martinis
- ☒ Living free and wild

I like to hold the hands of
- ☒ You
- ☐ Grandmothers
- ☐ Babies
- ☐ Aliens
- ☐ No one
If I were on a reality TV show it would be *Lifestyles of the poor and unappreciated*

Behind my mask I am
- ☐ warm and fuzzy
- ☐ ice clear to the middle
- ☐ on a spiritual mission
- ☒ wildly passionate
- ☐ I am my mask

Daisies,
the official flower
of the quirkyalone
movement.

be yours

international quirkyalone day:
february 14

International Quirkyalone Day is not anti–Valentine's Day.
It just happens to fall on the same day.

International Quirkyalone Day is a do-it-yourself celebration of romance, friendship, and independent spirit. There are no giant teddy bears, Hallmark cards, or gigantic red boxes of chocolate, just honest love and displays of affection for yourself, your friends, and a lover if you have one. The quirkyalone movement is a grassroots movement. Don't ask when IQD is coming to your

"How will I celebrate International Quirkyalone Day? I don't know, but it sure as hell isn't going to be like other February 14ths I've known—no vicious snarling at every person wearing red or carrying flowers. I will definitely buy daisies, at the very least. Maybe I'll paint the handle of my Hitachi Magic Wand bright purple." —Deirdre Moore, San Diego quirkyalone

Quirkyalones celebrate being single
Parties for growing movement held in eight cities

SAN FRANCISCO, Feb 15—As millions of American couples marked the Valentine's Day weekend with flowers and candle-lit dinners, a group of independent women who call themselves quirkyalones defiantly celebrated their lack of attachment.

Alone? Celebrate Anyway
How about anti-Valentine's Day? Or Quirkyalone Day? those are just some of the ways Americans are taking the sting out of being alone on Valentines Day. More . . . .

town; bring it there yourself. Declare a local soiree at a club or bar, or host a quirkyalone dinner party. Here are some suggestions from parties that got this holiday started in San Francisco, New York, Providence, and Glasgow, Scotland:

- An alone-time table
- A quirkyalone advice booth
- Crafts table for making quirkyalone cards
- Reading of inspirational quotes
- The classic party game in which you guess the name of the famous quirkyalone taped on your back by asking other party guests yes-or-no questions like "Am I alive or dead?" or "I know I'm a movie star, but is my hair really spiky and brown?"

FOR HOSTS: One fun thing to do is to circulate and ask people where they first heard about quirkyalone.

If you feel like celebrating the alone part of quirkyalone (as a single or a couple), here are some additional suggestions:

SINGLES
- Treat yourself to a day at a spa—bring a friend
- Dedicate a song to yourself on the radio
- Make yourself a quirkyalone mix tape
- Take a long drive and sing in the car

COUPLES
- Collaborate on a project
- Give each other back rubs
- Surprise your partner with a handwritten letter (or handmade anything)

EVERYONE
- Buy yourself a new vibrator
- Volunteer
- Plant a tree

· BIRTH OF a movement · BIRTH OF a movement · BITH

Quirky Quirky
yalone
quirky

ADVICE
BOOTH
5 CENTS

Reading your ... was
really important because it
made me see that I am not so
weird after all.
It reminded me that I can be
whole ... in myself, and th
as a ... musician,
most ... rk has
be ... le not ...
beg
Santa Cr...

QUIRKYALONE

Quirky' Day

By Dav...
CHRONICLE S...

S asha Cage...
she talks a...
Day. It is n...
tion you might ex...
gle woman of 29 ...
thrum of the day's ...

why Quirky? why Alone?

9-22-00

Dear Sasha Cagen
   I very much enjoyed yr article
"The Quirkyalone" as it appeared in the
Utne Reader. I read it at a perfect
time, after being dumped by my lover
of 6 months. I totally resonated with
your description of & ~~so~~ experience as a
quirky alone. I'm 43. never have had
a relationship that lasted longer than
3 years. I tend to go long periods
of time (sometimes years) between
relationships, often not even dating
anyone. (And I'm a lesbian on top
of everything else). Your line " there is
no patience for dating just for the sake of
not being alone" really hit the nail on
the head. And Rilke's "Letters" has often
been my bible. Reading yr article was
really important to me cuz it made
me see I'm not so weird afterall.

It reminded me that I can be whole + complete in myself + that, as a writer, musician, most of my best work has been produced while not in relationships.

Thank you— this has restored my pride in my solitude + singleness + reminded me that its OK.

Sincerely,
Patti Sirens
Santa Cruz
CA

P.S. I'd like to know if you ever do any further, research, studies, interviews, etc. on quirky alones

Name: Melissa Kirk

Age: 32

Hometown: Berkeley, Calif.

Current town: Berkeley, Calif.

Job: Acquisitions Editor for publishing company

Length of time quirkyalone: My whole life. My relationships have never fallen out the way society says they are supposed to. I've been a quirkyalone, quirkyslut, quirkyflirt, quirky-bitch, you name it.

Relationship status: Single

Personal QA motto: I believe I'm a beautiful, intelligent, kick-ass babe, and anybody who doesn't believe that doesn't get to see me naked!

Name: Tara Emelye Needham

Age: 30

Hometown: Lake Grove, N.Y.

Current Town: Albany, N.Y.

Job: Graduate Student, Ph.D English

Relationship Status: Single, nursing a broken heart from a recent break-up

Favorite Golden Girl: Rose

Favorite quirkyalone activities: Going to movies, rearranging furniture, running errands, journaling, long days at home with an endless cup of coffee

Personal QA motto: QA is about delighting in life, and the myriad relationships that connect us to the world and each other in meaningful ways.

Name: Bethany Cagen

Age: 24

Hometown: Cranston, R.I.

Current town: New York, N.Y.

Job: Program Manager for
a non-profit mentoring
organization

Length of time quirkyalone:
Full-fledged QA a few
years ago

Favorite quirkyalone activities:
Walking or biking alone in
quiet places with lots of trees,
giving myself pedicures while
watching cheesy television
shows, knitting, shopping in
thrift stores, making art projects, such as painting or crafts

Personal QA motto: To me,
quirkyalone is a way of life,
not just a relationship classification. Many people think the
term is weird when they first
hear it, and I think you can tell
a lot about someone by the
way they react. It's a way of
celebrating yourself and all
the possibilities life has to
offer. Above all, quirkyalone
is about embracing your
freedom to make choices.

Name: Steve

Age: 34

Hometown: Adrian, Mich.

Current town: Seattle, Wash.

Job: Independent Bookseller

Favorite Golden Girl: Bea
Arthur

Favorite quirkyalone activities:
Movies, rock 'n' roll shows,
book/CD shopping, biking,
listening to baseball on the
radio, drinking beer at my
local tavern

Mathematical Equation

Lived experience + innate nature = **quirkyalone**

chapter three
born or made?

The nature-versus-nurture debate is an ancient one, going back to the days of Plato and Aristotle. For those of us who spend so much of our lives single, one of the primary questions to consider is whether being quirkyalone is something that you *are* or something you *become.* Is this anti-dull-relationship stance combined with a love of independence an innate quality, or is it a result of certain choices and experiences? Why are some people just not comforted by a casual relationship and would rather hold out, even if it means staying single for eons?

I call myself a womb quirkyalone because even though intellectually I know that my quirkyalone status must be a complex combination of innateness and experience, it feels innate. I cannot imagine being any other way.

Not everyone feels that quirkyaloneness is inborn. In a national survey, about 65 percent responded that they belong to the womb subtype. The rest are what we call born-again quirkyalones. For born-again quirkyalones, coming out is more of an intellectual and personal growth process, a choice based on self-awareness and life experience. Sometimes born-agains experience an aha! moment, as Oprah might call it, but more often it is a dawning understanding, when they gradually realize a new approach to

Quirkyalone Thought to Ponder: "Neurotics are miserable because they think that they're not as good as everyone else. . . . Eccentrics know they're different and glory in it."
—David Weeks, author of a landmark study on eccentricity

life and love—after a divorce, traveling alone, through a spiritual awakening, or in a new plateau of adulthood.

There are similarities: each of us, whether womb or born-again, may have had a baptismal moment or a series of moments that blur into a feeling that quirky-aloneness is an expression of who we are.

COMING OUT AS A QUIRKYALONE

Whether you are a born-again or a womb, experience does play a role. In our first thirty years (and beyond) we receive all kinds of programming about the way our lives are supposed to be. To come out as a quirkyalone is to jettison those preconceived ideals in favor of the open road. It takes a certain leap of faith, to let your thoughts take you where they lead. You don't really know how it is going to turn out. But you know that you need to draw your road map for yourself.

The quirkyalone character develops out of an incubation period, a time of being single when you reach certain insights. Those insights then coalesce into a set of

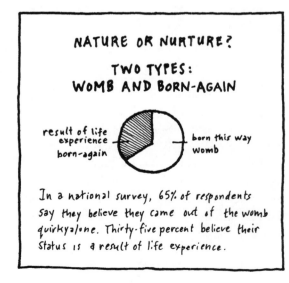

NATURE OR NURTURE?

TWO TYPES:
WOMB AND BORN-AGAIN

result of life experience born-again — born this way womb

In a national survey, 65% of respondents say they believe they came out of the womb quirkyalone. Thirty-five percent believe their status is a result of life experience.

ideas that you adapt and carry with you throughout the rest of your life—whether you are married, single, divorced, or widowed. When you are single long enough to know singleness is a unique state of being and not just a holding pattern between relationships, you are on the brink of becoming quirkyalone. Instead of becoming bitter, you start to question twenty-first-century cultural assumptions about love and romance. You wonder whether being coupled is always better than being single, you doubt that friendship should be a side dish to romantic relationships, and you question whether the traditional partnership is the only model for raising children and finding happiness. Quirkyalone is not just a phase—it's a worldview.

Just as there is an element of acceptance to the word *quirky*, as in accepting one's quirks, so coming out as a quirkyalone is a process of self-acceptance. It's not exactly like coming out as gay or lesbian, but it is a reckoning with your deepest self, your aloneness; it is a continual inner dialogue. Whether you are womb or born-again, coming out means taking responsibility for your own happiness and recognizing that no other person will hold the key to all your future joy. It's the opposite of debutante-style coming out. Instead of announcing yourself as available to everyone, you announce that you are committed to yourself and available to individuals of your choosing.

SIGNS YOU ARE A WOMB

Most womb quirkyalones have a sense, from an early age, of being different. It's common, though not universal, for wombs to have childhood memories of liking to be alone, playing alone, reading alone, amusing themselves with fantastic

"I've always known that I'm not a typical quirkyalone—I did go to prom, I always had boyfriends, I was a cheerleader. But there's a certain point when you realize, I'm not one of those people who is going to talk about weddings and babies all the time. I'm in a couple, but I don't want to be around that tyranny-of-coupledom mind-set."
—Danielle Jatlow, born-again quirkyalone

imaginations.* Matthew Rodriguez, twenty-four, traces his first memories of quirkyaloneness to the ages of four to six: "I would pack my favorite Madonna memorabilia and T-shirts into a little suitcase and fix myself some food to take to the end of the street or the backyard. Then I would sing and imagine."

Other womb quirkyalones point to high school as the essential period of incubation. For many women who grew up in suburbia or small towns, the smart-girl syndrome prevalent in all too many high schools is a factor. Like Ione Skye's valedictorian character in *Say Anything,* the introspective, analytic girl may be beautiful but not considered dating material. The same can be true for men: Eric Schiller, author of over one hundred books on chess, also sees his childhood intelligence as having played a role: "I've been a lifelong quirkyalone, created by the circumstance of skipping first grade."

Strong friendship bonds are also often cited as influential, almost as if your first friends are your first loves. Being so fulfilled by a group of friends or a particular friend in childhood, you learn friendship as the fundamental bond. Reyhan Harmanci says, "My friend and I have often talked about this. We think that in high school you become someone who socializes through friends and builds an identity from those friendships—or you have a serious girlfriend or boyfriend and that's how you relate to others. Long after high school, it's not hard to spot people continuing to socialize in similar ways."

Womb quirkyalones generally discover themselves as lovers later in life. But a feeling of alienation (however slight, not necessarily even painful) is almost constant. You can barely turn your head without seeing a billboard, a magazine cover, or a bus advertisement that reminds you that you exist on a different planet than most people. When you stand in the grocery checkout line, peering at the wall of women's magazines, you feel like an anthropologist looking for insights into another culture. When you do find yourself in a long-term romantic relationship, you may revisit these artifacts and smile, "Ahhh, this is what the women's magazines have been talking about."

---

*When you think about it, childhood is the original quirkyalone state: you don't *need* to have a romantic partner; you have friends. For children, the entire value system of quirkyalone—individuality, creativity, open-mindedness—is often natural and easy.

SIGNS YOU ARE A BORN-AGAIN

While for the womb it feels pointless to talk about the way you became quirkyalone because it's just the way you are, for born-agains it's the way you are now. In the past you may have been integrated into traditional dating scenes. You may have been a mad serial monogamist in college; you might have brought a boyfriend or girlfriend home every Thanksgiving. But for you, there's a process of coming to realize that you would rather be alone than in a stagnant relationship or even in a decent relationship that feels wrong or stifling. A key moment is when you realize that unless your potential date is going to be spectacular, you probably would prefer staying home to read a book. At least for a while, you stop dating as a sport.

In the past you may have harbored a secret pity for single people. You thought that being single was the worst possible fate. Then—in the wake of a breakup or even in the midst of a relationship—you realize that there are all these wonderful aspects to being single. During a long period of singledom (or separation from a lover), you start to savor all the time alone, the surplus energy for work and friends, and the exhilarating feeling of waking up unfettered. You discover the power of being alone with your thoughts and the pleasures of daydreaming, the freedom to do exactly what you want, when you want to do it. Often the longer you are single, the higher your standards grow.

Born-agains go through an interesting transition during this time, full of reflection on new approaches to life and love. Erica Jong sounds very much like a born-again quirkyalone in her midlife memoir, *Fear of Fifty*. She writes, "At nineteen, at twenty-nine, at thirty-nine, even—goddess help me—at forty-nine, I believed that a new man . . . would somehow change my inner life. Not so now. I know that my inner life is my own achievement whether there is a partner in my life or not. . . . I know that my soul is what I have to nurture and develop, and that, alone or with a partner, the problems of climbing your own mountain are not so very different."

"i've changed"

"Some quirkyalones are born smack-dab into it, but some, like me, I think, due to poor parental programming, lose their innate quirkyaloneness and have a hard road back to it—lots of fear, loathing, and loneliness because you don't understand what's missing. Especially for women of my generation, born in the early sixties, it was brainwashed out of you as a child. We're supposed to be wives, mothers, then, no, we're supposed to be free, single, empowered but make less than men.

"I left my first husband because he didn't respect that I was changing, but also because I became consistently attracted to men my own age who were very independent. I didn't want to be unfaithful, so I ended the marriage. This quirkyslut did have some sense of decency.

"But as is the way of life, all those available independent men disappeared the minute I became available, and my journey toward quirkyalone really began. It was nine years between marriages with a lot of bad and not-so-bad boyfriends. By the time I met my current husband, I had come to peace with the fact that it was cool and even better at times to be a quirkyalone and be choosy when I had quirkyflirting or quirkyslutty times. It was very empowering. When I met my husband, we clicked because he was a lot like me. I like being married (and I could only be married to another quirkyalone) because there is a calm-in-the-storm quality to it, and that—especially lately—is very comforting." —Beth Bachtold, 41

"i was born this way"

"I was raised by a lot of people to think that there was one path. If you didn't have a high school sweetheart to marry, you went to college to get one. I spent a lot of time in the late sixties and early seventies trying to find someone to shack up with and then eventually to marry. Looking back, I see it was counter to my basic instincts; it was like being gay, when the pressure is to marry the opposite sex. Then one day you admit it: 'I'm a quirkyalone, I was born this way' or 'I became this way,' and it doesn't matter. You are listening to yourself instead of whatever the outside messages are. You enjoy listening to yourself. I don't mean that you talk to yourself. But there's some inner dialogue, some inner calling that propels you forward. You never want to dilute that, diminish it, or sell it out. Therefore you would rather be alone than in a relationship that calls for losing your core sense of who you are." —William Poy Lee, 52

Now that we've named, defined, explained, and affirmed the quirkyalone, it's time for a little tough love. Let's be honest: there will always be lonely or embarrassing moments. We offer up this list of humiliating moments not to discourage or undermine quirkyalone values, but rather to say—you're not alone. Nothing like hearing about someone else's cringing moments to feel a little bit better about your own.

General social moments: When you are in the company of nonquirkyalones, and someone asks how long it's been since your last relationship. When you tell them, their jaws drop.

Wedding moments: Wearing a green bridesmaid dress or male equivalent.

Food moments: When the host or the hostess questions you loudly, "Just for one?" And the whole restaurant turns and looks. Yes, you are indeed eating by yourself.

Family moments: It goes without saying that at family gatherings, barbecues, weddings, funerals, and the like, you are going to be subject to pitying looks and squeezes on the arm, "Don't worry. It will all work out."

Dating moments: When it becomes clear to the person you are dating that you haven't dated in a while and your friends make such a big deal about it, "Oh, you're the one she has been talking about!" They treat your new significant other as if he/she is the second coming of Christ.

When a romantic interest says, "I Googled you," and you say, "I Googled you, too," and they say, "I was kidding."

"Coming out as a quirkyalone has reinforced my faith that while I am indeed 'eccentric,' this is nothing to hide. I read about the movement in *Utne Reader* in 2000, right before a ten-year Thanksgiving ritual was about to end. As a result of my childhood with an emotionally abusive stepmother, I dislike holidays and usually do something alone so I can reflect. For Thanksgiving I would always (1) be alone, (2) cook a big pot of spaghetti with ground beef and sausage, and (3) watch three movies. The first was always *When Harry Met Sally* (for its musings on possibilities of platonic friendships!). Earlier in the year I reunited with my real mother's family (after a twenty-one-year rift engineered by my stepmother) and returned for Thanksgiving. After reading the *Utne* reprint I vowed that I would not be ashamed if anyone asked about my ritualized solitary reflections (what I had done on previous Thanksgivings) and that I would continue them even if I became quirkytogether (and I have). Reading the article also reinforced my resolve to convince friends and family that I was not unhappy alone." —Walt Jacobs, 35

Name: Andrea Laurion

Age: 18

Hometown: Connellsville, Pa.

Current town: Allison Park, Pa.

Job: Right now I'm just a college student.

Length of time quirkyalone: I think I've been a quirkyalone since I was about twelve, if it's possible at that age.

Favorite Golden Girl: Sophia

Favorite quirkyalone activities: I love to go on walks, to find a nice-looking bench and just sit and watch people pass me by. I like to watch the way people interact with each other and sometimes I'll even make up stories for them.

Personal QA motto: I may look alone to the world, but with those I love I am fulfilled.

Name: Miranda Celeste Hale

Age: 24

Hometown: Spokane, Wash.

Current town: Spokane, Wash.

Job: Graduate student in English literature, teacher, writer

Personal QA motto: Red lipstick and a good book = the hottest date ever.

Name: C-Jay

Age: 50ish

Hometown: Cincinnati, Ohio

Current town: Washington, D.C.

Job: Yea I got one.

Favorite Golden Girl: Betty White

Favorite quirkyalone activity: Watering my fish

Name: Carolyn Dougherty

Age: 38

Hometown: Native Californian

Current town: Oakland, Calif.

Job: Civil engineer/professor/ railway historian

Relationship status: Currently monogamous with a man I've known nearly a year. We may marry next year to give him the right to work in the EU if he decides to join me in England.

Favorite quirkyalone activities: I could describe a few, but instead I'll just mention the one that is most important to me—exploring English country roads on my antique British motorcycle. It has to be England, it has to be an antique bike, and, most important, I have to be alone.

"Better to be untethered

and open

to possibility."

chapter four

when settling is not an option

A lot of people have the wrong idea about us. They assume that the "alone" part of our moniker means that we are totally content with being single; that our supreme comfort in singledom means we would never spy on a potential date, ask a friend to set us up, or use an online dating service. Actually, the truth is a bit more complex. We like being single, but that's not the only reason we spend such long periods in the single state. Our deeply romantic nature commands it—and creates a certain romance that can be equally possible in both coupled and single states.

Now, *romantic* is a tricky word. It seems worthwhile to point out that *romantic* as it applies to the quirkyalone is different from the romanticism presented to us in women's magazines and Hallmark cards. If we're going to be black-and-white about this, there are two kinds of romance: uppercase and lowercase. Lowercase romance is based on sentimentality and formula. It flattens meaning into a series of predictable gestures: sending flowers means "I'm thinking about you"; a marriage proposal in an Italian restaurant with a man playing violin means "I really love you." If you look even deeper into lowercase romance, you find commerce. The same industries that bring us all the rule books about women finding men exhort us to spend lavishly on weddings and

Quirkyalone Thought to Ponder: "We are all in the gutter, but some of us are looking up at the stars."—Oscar Wilde

Militant Romantic:

A person who holds out for ideals, even when the society at large says they do not exist.

"I want the spark, baby."
—Regina Edwards, 33

"Individuals who want to believe that true love does not exist cling to these assumptions because this despair is actually easier to face than the reality that love is a real fact of life but is absent from their lives."
—bell hooks, *All About Love*

—from Iowacity.com

honeymoons to prove the depth of our love. It's not that the quirkyalone is opposed to chocolate, diamond rings, roses, trips to Maui, or marriage proposals with men playing violin in the background. But we prefer gestures that feel more authentic (flowers any other day of the year than February 14). We also have our own spin on romance that sometimes is about amorous love and sometimes not.

When you are single for a while, you become more attracted to the meanings of uppercase *Romantic*. Uppercase Romantic is first and foremost about sincerity, but it also can take on the meanings of reverie, fantasy, introspection, intuition, and realness. For the quirkyalone there's a power in Romantic yearning—the stolid power in holding out for a vision, feeling a sense of possibility—but there's also a power in *not* yearning, in feeling self-contained. When quirkyalones are single, we tend to go back and forth between wanting a relationship in our lives and not really feeling the need at all. It can be possible to hang out with a couple that you like and not feel sad or jealous at all—just bask in their stability and be happy to go home unfettered to work on your own projects and sleep in your own bed diagonally. *Romantic* takes on yet another meaning here— the Romantic of large-scale emotion that is equally possible in a single state: the romance of walking down the street, being swept away by cheesy songs on your Walkman when you are very much alone, but in the best possible way. It's the sort of Romantic that makes you feel like you are starring in your own version of *Before Sunrise,* when you take a train trip by yourself. Just as you can dream of romancing a single person, you can enjoy the possibility of romancing the world in general (and yourself).

Quirkyalones are dreamers. In our healthiest, most evolved state, we expand the experience of falling in love or passionate interest beyond just one arena. A project can take as much time and energy as a "relationship." Maggie, a single mother in her forties, says the thing that struck her most in the original quirkyalone essay was the line "Better to be untethered and open to possibility." She was married, and it wasn't a horrible marriage, but "because I am a quirkyalone I couldn't be in it. My ex-husband is a wonderful guy, and we had problems, but I was suffocating because I couldn't be myself." She sees the quirkyalone part of her personality as connected to work and family life. "There's this expression, 'Boldness has genius, power, and magic in it,' by Goethe. I feel that— I do things my way and differently. I was a TV producer for fifteen years, having a very hard time being a single parent and working in this business. It looked like I was going to get laid off [along] with two hundred people. I decided to leave and write

Name: Shana Morris
Age: 33
Hometown: East Coast
Current town:
Albuquerque, N. Mex.
Job: Medical Records Clerk
and Bookseller
Length of time quirkyalone:
Always, except before this
year I usually got called
"weirdo."
Relationship status:
Terminally single
Favorite Golden Girl: Rose
Personal QA motto: "You
will do foolish things, but
do them with enthusiasm."
—Colette

Advice Corner

I'm worried that I have betrayed quirkyaloneness. Several times in the last week I have really wanted to date someone. I'm feeling guilty about the *desire* to date. Maybe it's because usually I feel like I am meeting new people, and now I go to a different house and it's always the same party, same people. At least if you are not dating someone you have that 'oooh, new people' thing. What do you think? —Brad

Dear Brad,

Dating (or wanting to date) does not make one a traitor to quirkyaloneness. It's the social obligation of dating that QAs fight, not the meeting-someone-you-want-to-spend-time-with part. Something in the tone of your note (perhaps the word *guilty*) makes me wonder if you think there is something wrong with taking initiative to improve your dating life. You may feel this is a betrayal of your core identity and fall into the trap of thinking that it's pathetic to take action in this realm. Meeting someone could happen magically: you could return a video, exchange glances with another customer, and then run into that person at a party a week later. But please, how often does that really happen? We wear a protective armor in public, and we often walk around in our own mental cloud. Taking steps to increase the chances of meeting new people is part of being a healthy quirkyalone, not a delusional one (who might secretly hope to meet someone by sending telepathic messages to someone across a crowded train).

full-time. Everyone thought that was a nice thing to do, like every other struggling writer, but I really did make a career out of it. People say all the time, 'How do you do it?' I don't know if resourcefulness is an aspect of being quirkyalone in terms of making things happen. That was a real hope and a dream—to have a lifestyle with my kids as I wanted. I loved the idea of not having to go to an office every day. It gave me a sense of being the underdog and making possibilities work for myself."

Still, it does seem a bit ironic that we would call quirkyalones—people who are rarely in *romantic* relationships—romantics. What do we know about relationships that others don't? We may have less experience than our serial monogamist friends, but what we do have, for better or worse, is a strong internal compass, a gut instinct that must be obeyed.

PATHOLOGICAL PICKINESS?

Just because we know this quality to be part of ourselves doesn't mean that we are always content with it. Anyone who holds out for years for an imagined ideal is bound to ask: Is it okay to follow my instincts, or is there something pathological and weird about me? What if I never find what I'm looking for? Am I going to become too set in my ways to accommodate anyone else? What if I'm wrong about it being braver to go it alone, and actually being in a relationship would be more courageous? What if I'm just wrong?

Every quirkyalone comes to a moment (or many moments) when she wonders if she is just pathologically picky. It doesn't help that the nonQA world looks at our dating patterns (or lack thereof) with a mix of bemusement and contempt, accusing us of holding out for a perfect hair day, the aligning of the planets, or the Messiah. We are often accused of being in love with love. We should go out on more dates, stop theorizing about love and start practicing it instead.

Yes, there are legitimate problems with escaping into fantasy for too long or for the sake of comfort. The momentum of quirkyaloneness can build: after one, two, three, or four years of assured singledom, it can become impossible to imagine getting involved again.

But the upside of being in love with love is maintaining a sense of hope and possibility. People think of romantics as soft, as people who are attracted to illusions. But Romanticism can also require a tough spirit—to be brave while all your cousins are getting married (even the ones who are ten years younger). It might be easier to follow convention and marry by the time you hit thirty-five or fifty or to continue on with a relationship for the sake of having a partner to calm nervous parents and a date to bring to weddings. But the alternative of "settling," a warm body for the sake of a warm body, makes us much more uncomfortable.

In this sense, quirkyaloneness is a choice. Quirkyalones are *militant* Romantics. It takes courage to keep holding out when you are told that you are holding out for an ideal that does not exist.

Most single QAs have not led celibate, loveless lives. We often have gotten a glimpse of the kind of relationship we are seeking, and such experiences intensify the desire to remain open to the possibility of finding a similar one. Most of us meet a person we're sure is a lifelong soul mate, who turns out to be anything but. If you are experiencing this trauma right now, I suggest immediately proceeding to page 55 to read about R.O., or romantic obsession. The quirkyalone's innate ability to experience a symphony of emotion may put you at risk.

Everyone has negative romantic experiences. The mark of a quirkyalone is that we don't let them get us down completely. We would rather be raw, take it, then move on. Of course, the quirkyalone heart can grow callused over time. Having high hopes leads to disappointment, and after many disappointments, when years go by and everyone else is paired off while we remain single, the hopeful nature of the quirkyalone can be worn away by a growing weariness and cynicism. Why bother investing hope again? It happens to the best of us. Cynicism and hope are always in flux.

What distinguishes the quirkyalone is that a kernel of hope lives on.

No one ever said that quirkyalone wasn't complex. It really is a paradox—the ability to be happy alone and still yearn.

TOUGH LOVE FOR QAs

Should she? Or shouldn't she? The question of whether to go on

ACCEPTING OR REFUSING
A DATE

a date or continue a relationship is charged for people like us; the all-or-nothing mind-set is hard-wired into the quirkyalone personality. We ardently desire the real thing and can't seem to deal with the casual or the imitation.

A few words of advice: every so often, push yourself. Force yourself out on the questionable date. The problem with all-or-nothing is that the all comes along so rarely that you may miss out not only on sex and companionship, but also on life itself. Quirky-alones want to know from the beginning that someone is "the one," or one of the "the ones," to feel stimulated and tingly, unique-ly understood. But of course sometimes people turn out to be different from what we originally expect.

Part of the challenge of dating is to manage the anxiety of letting a relationship unfold over time. The beginning of the relationship can be giddy, but it can also be excruciating. Ambiguity at the start is difficult for everyone, but for us it's especially hard. We want to call the question early—yes or no!—and retreat if things are not working immediately. Sayonara!

The challenge is to remember that unless you are developing a relationship with a friend, a co-worker, a church member, or a family member (probably not a good idea), getting to know someone is a gradual process. Friendships evolve over time, as do co-worker relationships and roommate bonds. Let's face it: the reasons we reject people can seem comical. One friend couldn't possibly go out with someone who asked her "to give him a buzz." Another no-no was the phrase "shoot me an e-mail."

"PRACTICE" RELATIONSHIPS

We're told that practice relationships are good. It's true that you do learn something in every relationship. But the difference between the quirkyalone and the serial monogamist is that we're a little reluctant to enter into relationships just for the practice. Of course, we don't want to be forty-six and in a relationship for only the third time, but we're not so sure we like the alternative either.

What happens most often is that someone wants to date you, you're not so crazy about that person, but you think that because everyone else is doing it, you should try it too. Attraction can build over time, right? Sometimes practice relationships work out fine. But sometimes when we force ourselves into relationships that don't feel right, the time spent together can have a double quality, as if we are watching ourselves in a romantic comedy. Worse yet is the constant second-guessing about whether it's you or the other person. These relationships can be brutal on the quirkyalone spirit, and they rarely end well.

The big problem with practice relationships is that often they devalue sexual attraction in favor of other, supposedly more lofty, criteria such as security, comfort, or "the person is nice." When you are working too hard to be attracted to someone and that person's skin tastes like garlic and you're closing your eyes to an extremely hairy back (and that bothers you), it just makes you feel more lonely. If you are in a relationship to feel normal, don't feel bad about ending the relationship. Get out.

FATE? DESTINY? ONLINE DATING?

Quirkyalones are attracted to the idea of serendipity, the "cute meet" we secretly enjoy in romantic comedies. Online dating, of course, is the opposite of serendipity. It is intentional, rational, and businesslike, a way of meeting a lot of people at once. You could argue that it is serendipitous to find your true love on the Internet—who would have thought you both would be online and looking at the same time? But the quirkyalone, whether she admits it or not, wants a romantic narrative. We are prejudiced against online dating because we prize stories. We want our relationships to have a madcap, chance beginning (magic!) to tell friends and ourselves later on. Let's face it, which would you prefer: (a) "We met online" or (b) "Funny you should ask, we accidentally swapped bags last year when I was coming back from visiting my family"?

Then again, it's highly unlikely that any of us would break up with someone we genuinely like with the excuse "I'm sorry, I met you online and I just can't seem to get over that."

Given the choice between meeting someone you like and not meeting anyone at all, well, perhaps it would be better for those who are earnestly looking for love to reexamine their prejudice. When you dig a little deeper, there is always a story to tell. Both of my parents met new spouses through the old-fashioned newspaper personal ads. The fact that they met that way is charming. Perhaps the story is about all the resistance you as a quirkyalone had to fight to write your profile.

There can be advantages. Some quirkyalones may prefer online dating. You can get to know each other in a gradual way. You can find out if your quarry shares your love for Wittgenstein or would be interested in hiking the Appalachian Trail with you. And if you think about online dating as an adventure, the opportunity to travel without leaving home, it's quite compatible with our personality. We're wanderers, adventurers. Why not break out of the narrow confines of the social circle you already inhabit? One of my two successful online dating experiences was with a young Swiss mathematician. We spoke French and ate at a French

West African restaurant. Honestly, the whole weekend felt like a low-cost trip to Europe.

If you're curious, do try online dating. Choose the site that most closely matches your personality, and approach the experience as a strategic tool, a jump start for life in general. You may not meet anyone you like in your round of coffee or drinks, but if you write an effective ad you cannot help but develop a glow, a certain je ne sais quoi. I call it the "personals prom queen effect." Suddenly the whole word is begging to go out with you.

Here are some more do's and don'ts for quirkyalones (or anyone) considering online dating:

do cut to the chase and meet for a drink or coffee after no more than a week of e-mailing. Meeting someone in person is entirely different from exchanging coy e-mails—and you're better off getting to know the real person before you become attached to the virtual counterpart.

do have a friend help you write your online profile. She or he can help you think of charming details, like the fact that you know how to prepare brussels sprouts that everyone loves or the fact that you can sing the entire score of *Oklahoma!* from memory.

do set up an alter-ego e-mail account. No need to compromise your privacy.

do accept that you may meet a lot of people you don't like much. It may take time to meet someone that you want to keep seeing—a problem for quirkyalones, since we tire easily

Name: Margo Montoya

Age: 30

Hometown: Arvada, Colo.

Current town:
San Francisco, Calif.

Job: Unemployed

Length of time quirky-
together: forty-three days

Relationship status:
Sharing bed but not
having sex

Favorite Golden Girl: The
really old one

Favorite quirkyalone
activities: Bookstore-going,
junk-food-eating,
video-renting

Personal QA motto: Not
single, individual

of dating. Do stop online dating before you get bitter about it. It's a numbers game; in all likelihood, you will have to meet *a lot* of people to find someone with whom you click. One workshop on the personal ads advises that on average you have to meet (not just correspond or talk on the phone with) thirty people before you find someone you want to keep seeing.

don't be afraid of becoming friends with someone you meet through your ad. If you like each other but don't feel that spark, there's no reason not to transition into a platonic relationship.

do consider carefully whether you should bother with speed-dating, that gulag of meeting and greeting, wherein you conduct whirlwind three-minute conversations with about twenty-five people in one night. The chances of meeting another quirkyalone, or another quirky person, at such an event are not great—how could they be, in such a sterile, regimented environment? It goes without saying that you also should not expect to find a QA soul mate on a reality-dating show.

do rejoice in your horror stories. They are the modern-day equivalent of war stories, badges of honor for navigating the often-absurd terrain of dating. Briefing your friends after a deliciously awful encounter can make it all okay.

THE DARK SIDE OF THE QUIRKYALONE: ROMANTIC OBSESSION (R.O.)

It's a little-known fact, but quirkyalones, for all their independence, also have a tendency to be swept away when they get close to love. We are passionate, romantic characters, and that click happens so rarely that the hunt for a partner can take on the character of a search for a holy grail. If you meet someone who stirs your interest only once every two years, it is bound to be an epic event. If things don't go according to plan, or even if they do, well, this can be difficult. We sometimes plunge into romantic obsession, or R.O.

R.O. is a distinct emotional experience: the dark side of the quirkyalone's passionate character, and our dirty little secret. R.O. is not unique to quirkyalones, but we are more likely to dip into this troubling state than are people who are more flexible in their search for love and therefore date more frequently. R.O. generally comes in the wake of a short-lived relationship, when you are trying to uphold an illusion about the relationship and the rest of your life is not in order. The beloved is unavailable in some way. There might be a one-in-a-million connection, but reality (geographic distance, emotional unavailability, or the annoying fact of one party already being married or involved) stubbornly intrudes.

In the wake of meeting someone who fulfills all our desired soul-mate qualities and yet does not deliver on his or her soul-mate potential, the quirkyalone goes through a crisis. A great gulf opens up between the contentedly single quirkyalone and the fixated one, who keeps replaying the same cinematic image from the beginning of the relationship over and over again.

Of course that picture becomes more complex, if, over time, a real relationship develops. But if "the relationship" is thwarted by awkward logistics, the initial image becomes fixed, like a record repeating. We all see the potential of that relationship held in one moment, and we can't forget it.

You are not necessarily in love, because there hasn't been enough time.

But still, there is a death, the death of a dream, a possibility. R.O. is an addiction, a way to remain close when the relationship is over. It's an expression of disbelief that the relationship could be over. As you experience R.O., you are conscious that your behavior is self-destructive, but you're totally engulfed by the emotion and can't leave until you are ready.[1]

You must grieve.

R.O. is also about being valiant, willing to make sacrifices for love, even when rationally the relationship is not love at all. All appropriate romantic comedies are put into service as templates of experience. The patron saint, the ultimate, the gold standard, is, of course, Lloyd Dobler (as played by John Cusack) in *Say Anything.* Once I was utterly convinced that I should be the female Lloyd—not quite holding a boom box outside my beloved's window, blasting "In Your Eyes" by Peter Gabriel, but still willing to go that extra mile, even to travel thousands of miles to show up at his door. The big problem is that Lloyd can get away with his stalker moves because he is male. A woman standing under someone's window late at night would come off as Glenn Close in *Fatal Attraction.* This inherent unfairness is perhaps one more reason that female quirkyalones persist in R.O. behavior long after such grand gestures have stopped getting

John Cusack in *Say Anyt[...]*
patron saint of romantic obses[...]

us anywhere; in the warped mind of someone deep in R.O., the willingness to contemplate such gestures almost becomes a blow for women's rights: equal-opportunity stalking!

Are R.O.s all bad? Well, they aren't great. One does not necessarily want to go through dozens of R.O.s in a lifetime. They can be emotionally exhausting, they often alienate your friends, and if you are scarred too many times, you can just get worn down and cynical. Many of our friends do not understand the lengths to which we can go in R.O.—the months we spend dissecting the end of the relationship, the way we continue to track someone's behavior even when the breakup is ancient history. It can be bewildering for us too, seeing as this tempest of emotion stands in such contrast to our staunchly held image of confidence and self-reliance.[2]

A few years ago I was in the grips of an R.O. that, thankfully, was my last (we do tend to decrease the frequency of these outbursts with age, thank the Lord). I went to the Internet in search of insights. I punched those two words into Google. In an essay, "Obsessive Love," Hakim Bey writes, "The emergence of Capitalism exercises a strange effect on romance . . . as if the Beloved becomes the perfect commodity, always desired, always paid for, but never really enjoyed." Since we do not seem to be on the verge of socialist revolution, we may have to deal with the by-product of R.O. for a while. The following list of diagnostic signs and remedies should help.

help!

[1.] R.O. can be used as a verb to say that "you are R.O.-ing over someone." A more common usage is as a noun: "One falls into a state of R.O."

[2.] Note that it's also possible to be in a state of R.O. while in a relationship. This stunted form of romance often occurs in the first few months while you are captive to a constant, running analysis of the relationship. You bounce between extremes: This is great! This is doomed! When you are free of R.O., you can enjoy each other, and if there are issues, you talk about them. To be in a relationship free of R.O. is the mark of a real relationship. Ahhhh. A wonderful thing.

R.O. Checklist:
Diagnostic Signs

R.O. certainly can lead to some rather surprising behavior. After years of experience, I understand the dichotomy between the self-assured quirkyalone and the swooning, porous romantic inside, and I am prepared to help you. The following list contains clues that you too may be in the throes of an R.O. Review the checklist. If you have engaged in two or more behaviors, proceed to the "Remedies" section.

Excessive Googling. In the Internet age, the number one symptom of R.O. It's one thing to Google the object of your affection once or twice after you first meet, but if you find yourself re-Googling every day to see if there is a new link, or Googling his or her friends and family, consider that you may have a problem.

Compulsive phone behaviors. Checking phone messages, making excuses to stay at home to wait for a phone call, and calling your own phone to make sure it's working. All clues.

Forwarding e-mails or voice-mails for examination by others.

Drunk-dialing.

Major over-romanticizing. Turning past moments together into a movie (not the good kind, either). The cheesiest fuzzy-camera movies, in which the same romantic moment happens over and over again. Imagining yourselves as a cute elderly couple, telling people how you first met, à la *When Harry Met Sally.*

Obsessive discussions with friends that test everyone's sanity. It always starts with a disclaimer: "Really, I'm not going to talk about this again, but do you think that when he said, 'I'll call you later,' he meant, 'I'll call you later tomorrow' or 'I'll call you later in life'? Or maybe he meant I should just call him." Quirkyalones are creative types. This creativity can be deployed to find meaning in the most casual of interactions.

"Without obsession, life is nothing." —JOHN WATERS

Breaking things off early because you feel threatened by your own interest. And then obsessing about the person anyway.

Talking to strangers about the beloved. Combing through your address book to find old friends who have not heard the story yet. Talking to your mother about R.O.

Coming up with bizarre excuses to go to the beloved's neighborhood. As a quirkyalone, you are in denial and don't want to admit that you are a stalker.

Rehearsing speeches, the big ones about the demise of the relationship and even the "Hey, what's up?" or the "Hey, how are you?" speech.

Overly dramatic accusations. In your head, so much has already gone on between you.

Trying to worm your way into the beloved's social circle. Cultivating friendships that you honestly would not want unless you were trying to get close to that person.

Going to a department store to sniff the beloved's perfume or cologne.

Remedies As a quirkyalone, you are attracted to melancholy. Enjoy it. It's classic romantic behavior. But now you've felt all there is to feel, you've bored your friends to death, and now Mr. or Ms. Wonderful has caller ID or a cell phone with an Ignore button. Now is the time to collect your dignity and move into another state of mind. Everything up to now was about your future together. Now it is time to embrace a new vision, with just you as the romantic lead. Here are some strategies:

Cut off communication. In obsession, you perceive only part of reality. You really don't know the object of desire, at least not in totality or in his or her current state. Confronting the person and continuing a dialogue helps only if it helps you see the person for who he or she really is. If you are not experiencing relief from talking, stop. No more e-mails, voice-mails, or text messaging!

Embrace clichés. There is nothing wrong with you, nothing you could have done differently. You can't change someone. Real love doesn't feel like this. This really wasn't meant to be. *Let go and let God.* Repeat these end-of-the relationship affirmations to yourself, and then . . .

Place a personal ad. Even if you don't go on any dates, you'll feel better knowing that there are other fish in the sea.

Explore extreme dislike. Rejection is much easier to deal with when you can hate the offending party. (This may or may not be true, but it does seem to be an unavoidable and oddly satisfying part of R.O. recovery.) Pick one visceral moment of dislike—recall an insensitive comment he or she made, or one that involves the five senses (they say smells generate the strongest memories). Meditate. Then take out a piece of paper and list the beloved's unappealing characteristics. (See page 61, "Dated Then Hated.")

Befriend your diary. When you are in the throes of an R.O., go back and read some of your old entries. You may be able to recognize a pattern; with the knowledge that past beloveds were not all you cracked them up to be, you may be better able to cut the current R.O. short. Either way, the best remedy is to continue writing in your diary. The feelings are powerful and cannot be denied. Express it all in words. Months later you'll be able to go back and see the light.

Smile inwardly. Remember that running into the subject of an R.O. years later can be extremely satisfying. You will probably realize that the person is far more annoying/arrogant/slimy/skinny than the fantasy image you constructed. When you see the people he or she dated after you, you realize that he or she is with the girlfriend or boyfriend that you as a quirkyalone would never want to be. Wow, you really did want someone to give up his or her identity completely to be with you!

Wash your sheets.

Obviously, you can always find someone new to obsess about. But I didn't say that.

DATED THEN HATED

At the opposite end of the spectrum from R.O. is the syndrome of Dated Then Hated, a condition from which quirkyalones also suffer. Quirkyalones have high hopes, and, obviously, high hopes can lead to disappointment. How is it that so often someone who seems a bona fide enlightened, funny, and singular person—someone you can see no reason not to be interested in—turns out to be altogether different when push comes to shove? Why does what you see in potential partners so often not translate into what you get? Of course, some of the responsibility rests with our own shortsightedness, the lovesick myopia that refuses to read the signs that people put out, and the intensity of emotion that we feel in general. But, you have to admit, part of the problem is that there are simply a lot of love criminals out there, and sometimes we don't recognize them as the emotionally disabled jugglers they are until it's too late.

We've all moped about this sorry state of affairs, but moping gets you only so far. By naming the problem, we at least can alert each other to these ten most commonly encountered types and the behavior their cool exteriors hide. Henceforth, these charlatans will be tagged with a label: DTH—Dated Then Hated. Manipulative, pathological, big-eater slobs will never sleep soundly again.

The dated-then-hated experience can happen at any age, but it is a rite of passage for young quirkyalones. Unpracticed in the ways of love, the young QA has not yet learned that there are love criminals on the loose.

WHAT YOU SEE	WHAT YOU GET
European Intellectual/Filmmaker	Financially dependent, big-eater slob
Sensitive Writer	Mr. Party Guy who goes out with blonde androids
Shy Poet	Incapable of eye contact, pathological coward
Middle-aged Bookworm	Virgin
Cool Indie Rock Boy	Most self-conscious person on Earth, with negative sex drive
Left-wing Journalist	Self-absorbed, fascinated with himself, cheats on girls and lies, and really gets around
Dot-Com Guy	Dot-Com Guy
Critical Theory Guy	Really, really, really bad in bed
Mild-mannered Teddy Bear	Weird, hairy monster who dials 900#s at night for fun
Feminist	Robert Bly in disguise

Insert yours here.

Le quirkyslut

How does sex fit into the quirkyalone picture? Put another way, how do we de
with the fact that we can go months or even years outside of a committed romant
relationship while still being human (with wants and needs!)? In decades pas
women who failed to marry were assumed to lack a sex drive. By now, however,
should be clear that there is no link between being single (or quirkyalone) an
being celibate.

It's impossible to make a generalization about the sexual behavior of a
quirkyalones. Some people live happily without sex for months and years. (Ofte
when you don't have sex for a while, you eventually forget what all the fuss wa
about.) Some people recycle exes. Some people develop friends-with-benefits rela
tionships. Some master the art of solo sex.

Sometimes we are single, and we do want action with another human being. The
what happens? The quirkyalone puts on a new pair of sunglasses, a new outlook o
life, a new attitude. We call that new lens Le Quirkyslut.

Quirkyslut is a term of personal empowerment and independence. It underscores th
point that you don't need to be in a serious, long-term relationship to explore you
sexuality. Sleeping with someone you've only recently met or making out with
stranger on a trip to Japan doesn't make you a slut; it makes you a quirkyslut, on
who continues to have high standards for a romantic relationship but is more flex
ible for a Saturday (or even Tuesday) night encounter.

Now, it's tricky to call someone a slut. Some people don't respond well to this bol
language, but the point is that we can reinvent words to take the sting out of then
The quirkyslut uses sex not to snare men or to boost her self-esteem, but becaus
she or he wants to explore and have fun, to experience the bodily pleasures avai
able to us. She is unashamed of her sensuality and unabashed about going for wh
she wants.

Full-time quirkysluts may need sex on a regular basis. They start to twitch if the
go without for several months or even several days. (See Samantha Jones of *Se
and the City* and Blanche Devereaux of *The Golden Girls*.) Full-time quirkyalones an

"My sex life is not dependent on my love life." —"Marcia," quirkyslut

usually able to weather life without sex for a while. But then they might enter a quirkyslut phase. The world becomes a much more sensual place, and sex takes on greater importance. The quirkyslut comes in waves (pun totally intended) for most of us, as we go back and forth between quirkyalone, quirkyslut, quirkyalone. One week being alone and chaste is wonderful. The next week the exact opposite is true. We want to make out with three people in line at the post office.

The quirkyslut often emerges during travel. We're not talking about participating in sexually exploitative tourism but rather referring to the fact that when we depart from our daily routines we are likely to find ourselves in a more liminal, sexually expressive state. With little chance of running into a new partner at the local café the following day, we feel, shall we say, more liberated. It's much cleaner to hook up with someone in a foreign city, or even across the state line, than to have a one-night stand in your own bedroom, where your partner sees the actual you and leaves the residue of his or her existence in your life. A new environment gives you the permission to be someone else, and desires that ordinarily would not be contemplated may be quite easily indulged.

QUIRKYALONE	QUIRKYSLUT
Lives in the future (as far as sex is concerned)	Lives in the moment
Inhabits the home	Often emerges during travel
Sex and love go together	Better able to separate sex and love
High standards for romantic relationship	High standards for romantic relationship/more flexible for Saturday night encounter
Generally a lifelong orientation	Generally a mode that we move in and out of depending on other factors such as stress level, hormones, and the weather
High self-esteem	High self-esteem: we're not engaging in this behavior because we don't feel loved by our parents. We're doing it to explore and have fun.
Puts a positive spin on something that previously had been scorned	Ditto

GREAT QUIRKYSLUTS IN HISTORY

Margaret Sanger: Indicted for inciting violence and promoting obscenity when she founded the modern American birth control movement.

Erica Jong: Has written frankly about female sexuality since the publication of the sexual-revolution classic *Fear of Flying* in 1973; coined the phrase "zipless fuck" to refer to an ideal of no-strings-attached, casual sex.

Blanche Devereaux (Rue McClanahan): A saucy, self-proclaimed slut who defied viewers' stereotypes of life in middle and old age on *The Golden Girls.* **Choice dialogue:**

> **Blanche:** I never tell a man about my past.
> **Rose:** Why not?
> **Blanche:** Because it takes so long.

Helen Gurley Brown: *Sex and the Single Girl* doesn't sound like a radical title now, but it was in 1962. Brown made a radical statement for her time in acknowledging that single women do have sex lives and that they can be as fulfilling as a traditional marriage.

Helen Gurley Brown, at work in her Park Avenue apartment, 1965

Nola Darling (Tracy Camilla Johns): The heroine of Spike Lee's 1986 *She's Gotta Have It* is a quirkyslut in a conundrum: a smart, sexually adventurous, independent woman struggles with being in simultaneous sexual relationships with three men. All three men want her to commit solely to them; Nola resists being "owned" by a single partner.

Dan Savage: Sometimes mean, generally fair, always willing to research obscure questions. He speaks for the sinners in his books and advice column for the gay, straight, and confused.

Betty Dodson: In the early seventies even *Ms.* magazine refused to publish her article on female masturbation for fear of offending readers. She self-published instead, and *Sex for One: The Art of Self-Loving* went on to become a multimillion-copy best-seller. Now in her seventies, she writes in her latest book, *Orgasms for Two: The Joys of Partnersex*, about a surprising and fulfilling sexual relationship with a twentysomething male partner.

Quirkyalones have vibrators.

"I'm a married quirkyalone (my mate is a quirkyalone as well) who has a history of quirkyslutness. The quirkyslut thing is a lot about my not really believing in monogamy as the only state of being—although I practice it. My history as a quirkyslut had a lot to do with personal empowerment and independence. I am still an unabashed flirt—quirkyflirt, if you will." —"Fiona," quirkytogether/quirkyslut

---

"I've decided I am not going to hold back from having sex. What, and wake up in five years and regret that I passed my sexual prime so I could wait for a guy who would 'respect' me for not having sex on the first date? I don't have time to be living in the Victorian days. I now see what is going on with older women and younger men because I have experienced it firsthand. The younger guy can keep up with the sexual insatiableness that many older women feel in their late thirties and early forties. It lends itself to the potential of having sex for hours."

—"Brenda," quirkyslut

QUIRKYSLUT HISTORY

In the nineteenth century the most common female malady was "hysteria," a medical term to describe a woman's display of mental or emotional distress. It may surprise readers to learn that treatment for hysteria was often a visit to the doctor for a manual massage of the vulva in order to induce "hysterical paroxysm" (better known as orgasm). But according to Rachel Maines, author of *The Technology of Orgasm: "Hysteria," the Vibrator, and Women's Sexual Satisfaction*, the manual massage was a "job that nobody wanted." Doctors often found this responsibility burdensome and sought various ways of avoiding the task — sometimes delegating the chore to midwives, sometimes employing mechanical devices. An American doctor patented the first steam-powered vibrator in 1869. Eventually these devices became battery and electric powered, available for purchase and home use. Perhaps all those hysterical women were not sick at all. They were simply budding quirkysluts, getting their needs met.

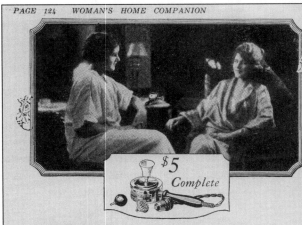

en nineteenth-century doctors tired
he task of stimulating their "hyster-
' patients to orgasm, they turned
mechanical devices for help. Ads for
ators became common in many
azines as women purchased them
home use. Marketed as cure-alls for
anging from headaches to asthma
even tuberculosis, the vibrator's
ulness for masturbation was never
nowledged. But quirkysluts must
e known the truth. As one vintage
ertisement claims, "almost like a
cle is the miraculous healing force
assage when rightly applied."

1. How to Start.

...p in Both Hands to Test
...gth of Current Before Ap-
...g to Other Parts of Body.

2. Wet Sponge.

Wet Sponge Extension Applicator Attached to Roller.

3. Sponge and Roller.

Extension Applicator Attached to Barrel. General Faradization of Neck or Throat.

4. Roller, Muscle Massage.

Can be Applied to Arms, Breast and Muscular Parts of Body.

...oller, Vertebral Massage.

...ning Roller Up and Down
Spinal Column.

6. Sponge and Roller.

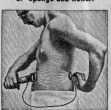

Massaging Bowels and Intestines.

7. Spinal Massage.

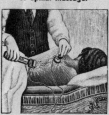

Spinal Massage Applied by Attendant.

8. Electric Hand Massage.

Very Pleasing to Some People. Electricity and Personal Magnetism.

...oncentrated Application.

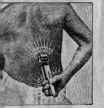

Faradizing a Joint.

10. Electric Bath.

Water and Electric Combination.

11. Scalp Brush.

Removal of Dandruff. Electric Scalp Massage.

Electreat and Accessories

According to legend, the unicorn symbolizes a
desire to work toward greater clarity in yourself,
and protection while you are on this search.

chapter five
Loneliness vs. solitude

Do quirkyalones get lonely? Of course. We all get lonely. Loneliness is hard to define because it is fundamentally about absence. It's the feeling that something is missing, even if you can't specify what: a romantic partner, a friend, a sense of confidence or place, a feeling of purpose. Loneliness is when you want the phone to ring and it doesn't. Your friends are not around, and even telemarketers do not love you. Loneliness is a fact of life, even though we don't want to admit it. A *Shape* magazine article reports that in anonymous polls, people own up to being lonely, but when asked to give their names, they change their answer to "self-sufficient."

Like everyone else, quirkyalones alternate between states of loneliness and solitude. One day we might be stirring spaghetti sauce for a solo supper, listening to public radio, and feeling that there could be no better companion than a review of a new novel and our reaction to it. The next night we might be doing the very same thing, but this time we feel a powerful aching need for someone else to be there. If loneliness is about lack, solitude is the opposite, a feeling of being whole, sometimes deliriously so. Solitude is taking pride in knowing that you are able to amuse yourself, take care of yourself, or being deliciously lost in your own thoughts,

Quirkyalone Thought to Ponder: "Language has created the word *loneliness* to express the pain of being alone, and the word *solitude* to express the glory of being alone."
—Theologian Paul Tillich

painting, writing, or organizing files for hours on end. Sitting alone in a messy living room surrounded by dirty teacups and emptied-out ice cream containers feels lonely, while doing something as simple as putting new shoelaces in your shoes or paying your bills on time (if you ordinarily have trouble with that) or cleaning your house can feel oddly fantastic.

There's something key about this distinction, as if when we are lonely we are vanquished, but when we feel solitude we are victorious. This is not just a matter of turning a frown upside down or making lemonade out of lemons or making do with being single as the next-best alternative because, as we all know, you can be lonely in a relationship too.

At some point in our lives we all confront the reality that each of us is ultimately alone. Perhaps part of the *quirky* in *quirkyalone* involves engaging in a dialogue with this aloneness. Lindsey, twenty-nine, says, "For me, one of the important things to experience in being single for a long time is that you are afraid, and you are forced to give up the illusion [that a relationship is the answer]. The human dilemma becomes really real for you. One of the reasons we crave partnership so much is it's the spiritual quest. Because part of the human condition is to be separate, we are all looking for connection. Religious people might find their relationship with God, and in the material world we are looking for that salvation in a romantic relationship. It's never going to be all that."

Exploring our aloneness does not mean hiding in a cabin in Montana; it means careful self-reflection, and it actually can put us in a stronger position to interact with other human beings. In *Letters to a Young Poet*, quirkyalone patron saint Rainer Maria Rilke nails why: "It becomes always clearer that this is at bottom not something that one can take or leave. We *are* solitary. We may delude ourselves and act as though this were not so. . . . But how much better it is to realize that we are so, yes, even to begin by assuming it. . . . Only someone who is ready for everything, who excludes nothing, not even the most enigmatical, will live the relation to another as something alive and draw exhaustively from his own existence."

But that is the heavy part of being alone. In some ways, spending time alone is just not a big deal for people like us. It's part of life. Sometimes spending time alone is just fun—and absolutely necessary for sanity's sake. Solitude is the kind of thing you don't even appreciate until it's gone. When you go home for the holidays or find yourself in a new, intense relationship, you realize that you need a certain amount of time alone or you start to twitch. Being alone is the only way to be creative in many disciplines. It's when we are alone that we are able to allow our thoughts to take shape. You don't need to go on a Buddhist retreat to be in touch with your "true self." Solitude often happens naturally, while we are walking around the city, drinking coffee, even while hiding out in the bathroom at work—just a bit of time alone, time for a mini–internal dialogue, allowing our thoughts to lead us where they will.

This is why walking alone is such a vital time for us: it's a convenient, incidental solitude. And in pop culture the woman walking alone is such a cliché image of romantic aloneness: in the opening scenes of *Felicity*, in *Ally McBeal*, in advertisements, and even at the end of *Shakespeare in Love*. We rely on stretches of walking-alone solitude—to think, regard buildings and the pastel sky, let thoughts bubble up inside of us—as a natural part of our days. It's a time for contemplation. The uncompromising honesty of the quirkyalone, her unwillingness to sell out or settle, comes from an almost compulsive conversation with the self. Should I stay in this job? Should I break up with him? Should I stick it out? Some people might say that examining one's life in such detail is neurotic, but for us it's part of mental health, part of living a life of integrity—keeping our actions consistent with our beliefs and ourselves.

Loneliness
When you want the phone to ring, and it doesn't.

Solitude
Walking alone, when a "little bomb of revelation" comes*

*According to Brenda Ueland, (profiled on page 123), author of *If You Want to Write*, a book that uses writing as a catchall term for all kinds of creative activity, long walks alone are one of the best ways to stoke the imagination. According to Ueland, there is never a long walk without a "little bomb of revelation," and it is often in walks that are a little too long that ideas come.

Deeply single:
A state of
perceiving the
benefits of
aloneness and
being single—
of traveling,
going to movies
alone, feeling full
of possibility.

Not every Friday night alone can be transcendent. Nor will every trip alone yield earth-shattering insight. There are definitely lonely times too, when aloneness feels like a gaping maw and you just wish that someone, anyone, would call you on the phone. But every quirkyalone knows that spending a weekend night by yourself is not necessarily pathetic. There can be odd joys of dancing alone in your bedroom or singing in the shower. I like to think of these moments as "glowful" because it helps me picture a candle in a window, something almost divine about drawing resources from yourself. Mary Wollstonecraft said it well in 1792 in *A Vindication of the Rights of Woman:* "Solitude and reflection are necessary to give to wishes the forces of passions, and to enable the imagination to enlarge the object, and make it the most desirable."

quirkyalone = flaneur, not loner

One common misconception about quirkyalones is that we are basically loners, the kind of people who don't like to socialize. In fact, we are usually a complicated mix of sociable and introspective. Often the solitary states we seek are those that put us in places of possibility. Walking alone, sitting in a café, or traveling on a train, we thrive on a mix of solitude and adventure. New people! We love to meet new people!

A term more precise for us than *loner* is *flaneur*. In *The Flaneur: A Stroll Through the Paradoxes of Paris,* Edmund Wilson describes a flaneur as "that aimless stroller who loses himself in the crowd, who has no destination and goes wherever caprice or curiosity directs his or her steps." The flaneur is a wanderer and observer, ambling through a city without apparent purpose but secretly in search of adventure

Inspirational (and Realistic) Quotes About Solitude

"There are days when solitude is a heady wine that intoxicates you with freedom, others when it is a bitter tonic, and still others when it is a poison that makes you beat your head against the wall." — Colette

"Everyone has a talent. What is rare is the courage to nurture it in solitude and to follow the talent to the dark places where it leads." — Erica Jong

"I am alone here for the first time in weeks to take up my 'real' life again at last. That is what is strange — that friends, even passionate love, are not my real life, unless there is time alone in which to explore and to discover what is happening or has happened."
— May Sarton, *Journal of a Solitude*

In the 19th century the consummate Parisian flaneur was the poet Baudelaire. He escribed flaneurs as people whose "independent, passionate, impartial minds . . . anguage can only awkwardly define." He also wrote, "The crowd is his domain, as he air is that of the bird or the sea of the fish. His passion and creed is to *wed the rowd.* For the perfect flaneur, for the passionate observer, it's an immense pleasure o take up residence in multiplicity, in whatever is seething, moving, evanescent and nfinite: you're not at home, but you feel at home everywhere. . . ."

How do most quirkyalones discover the flaneur in them? It often happens during ravel, exploring a new part of a city, crashing parties, or going out alone.

John, forty-two, writes, "I believe pretty strongly that you meet more people when ou are alone. If you are traveling as a couple you are walled off from those travel niracles." A woman shares that adventures can happen close to home: "Going out lone is the best. Single people get pulled into the best adventures. No one wants o approach couples to start a conversation or ruckus. I can't even tell you how many nsane things I've gotten involved with because I go out by myself."

We quirkyalones are lovers, but we are also flaneurs. Unless one person is really

FROM LONELINESS TO SOLITUDE:
Some Conversion Strategies

Eat well and exercise. Mom was right. You are what you eat. Sometimes the difference between solitude and loneliness can be as simple as taking care of yourself—eating well and exercising. Quirkyalones can drift so far away in our heads that we forget that we have bodies. (Even the flaneur, according to Wilson, can spend so much time wandering around the city that he forgets to eat.) We are more vulnerable to loneliness when we are famished or hungover, when bills are not paid and posture is bad. Essentially, you have to work at your relationship with yourself just as you would work at a relationship with another person. That means buying yourself flowers every so often, exercising and taking care of your body, and eating well (it's hard to reach solitary bliss when you consume only Diet Coke and pistachios). Also, stop checking your e-mail all the time. In addiction, no love is possible, for yourself or anyone else.

Watch dating shows. Conversely, when you really can't take care of yourself, when you are completely decimated by a week of work, when you don't have the energy even to call a friend, don't feel bad. Here's what you do: flip through the channels to find the cheesiest reality dating show possible, like *elimiDATE* or *Blind Date*, to remind yourself of how rarely a date leads to a love connection and how superior you can feel sitting on your couch at home. During commercials silently chant this quote from the movie *Election*: "People like you have to pay a price for being so great—and that price is loneliness."

SECRET SINGLE BEHAVIOR

Eating peas out of a can while walking around the apartment naked. Watching infomercials from 9 P.M. until midnight. A term coined on the hit HBO series *Sex and the City*, secret single behaviors are the idiosyncratic, sometimes embarrassing rituals you develop over years of singledom, rituals that are hard to give up when another person enters your life and your domain. Making the transition to a romantic relationship when you have a lot of SSB can be challenging, but let's be real: when life is this fantastic, who needs a romantic relationship?

Partial List of SSBs *(list could be endless)*

- Singing the chorus of a classic pop song (example: "Holiday") over and over again
- Downing a whole bag of salt-and-vinegar potato chips
- Letting your kitchen sink turn into a swamp
- Cutting your toenails on the kitchen table and leaving them there
- Getting stoned, reading a book in bed, being totally amazed by how profound every line is—how did they ever write that? Bonus points for eating chocolate chip cookie dough ice cream at the same time
- Practicing dance moves in front of the mirror before going out
- Making strange food concoctions, for example, spaghetti with beans on top
- Rearranging furniture weekly
- Trimming leg hair while listening to the radio
- Creating piles of dandruff while rereading your diary in bed
- Foot-picking

Favorite Quirkyalone
Activities (compiled from
a national e-mail survey)

Working out
Having coffee in a
  coffee shop
Cooking
Long walks
Sitting in the park
People-watching
Reading
Traveling on your
  own/Hopping trains
Exploring a new part
  of town
Checking out new artists,
  musicians, venues
Hours by the ocean
Meditating
Baking bread
Lying on the couch with
  a good book
Cooking brunch for
  friends
Renting movies that no
  one else wants to see
Going to the movies alone
Looking at fruit trees in
  a nursery
Dancing around the
  apartment in boxers
Singing in the mirror
Cleaning
Smoking cigarettes while
  doing the dishes
Walking aimlessly through
  the streets, by night
  and by day (they are
  totally different
  experiences)
Talking to strangers
Flying kites
Organizing/Filing
Writing letters
Going to a museum alone
  and taking a long time
  to look at everything
Paying bills in a public
  place, like a café

GOING TO THE MOVIES ALONE

If you're having trouble reconciling yourself to the horror of going to a movie alone, try this Mad Libs–style exercise first. Or take it with you. To begin, simply fill in the blank spaces below. (DO NOT LOOK AT THE STORY FIRST!) Then, using the words you have chosen, fill in the blanks in the story, and read aloud. Voilà: fun!

adjective _____
verb _____
adjective _____
color _____
insect(plural) _____
mammal (plural) _____
celebrity _____
same celebrity _____
farm animal _____
adjective _____
same adjective _____
noun _____
adverb _____
farm animal _____
power tool _____
adjective _____
adjective _____
adjective _____
same celebrity _____
noun _____

GOING TO THE MOVIES ALONE

After a _____ (adjective) day at work, I really needed to

_____ (verb). Flipping through the _____ (adjective)

Daily Gazette, I saw that _____ (color) was playing. "God, I am

such a sap," I thought. "I love movies about _____ (insect, plural)

falling in love with _____ (mammal, plural). All my friends

were busy, so I had to dig deep into my soul, and ask if I wanted to go

to the movies alone. Momentarily, I wavered. I asked myself what

_____ (celebrity) would do. Yes, I grinned to myself, of course,

the answer is obvious. Thinking again of _____ (same celebrity),

I put on a touch of the scent of _____ (farm animal), and hit the

road. Traveling to the cinema, I started to feel really _____ (adjective).

At the ticket counter, I felt even more _____ (same adjective). I had

to say, "One for _____ (noun)." He repeated "Only one?"

"Yes," I said _____ (adverb). Scanning the theater for a seat, I

realized that I was going to be the only _____ (farm animal)

on my own in the room. I saw another solo person and began to sit down

when he said, "Sorry, no, that seat is saved for my _____ (power tool)."

Luckily, there was one _____ (adjective) empty seat three

rows down. Though it was hard to withstand everyone's _____

(adjective) looks, I felt _____ (adjective) about my choice.

As the previews started, I smiled in the dark knowing that _____

(same celebrity) would approve of my amazing _____ (noun).

marry yourself first:
The mini-trend of self-matrimony

Remi Rubel officiates at her own wedding (as an ordained minister of the Universal Life Church).

Self-marriage isn't exactly a growing trend (no women's magazines have covered it, as far as I can tell), and it's definitely not a required behavior for quirkyalones. But marrying oneself is a sign of the times. Flipping on the radio, I happened to tune into voice-over artist Debi Mae West (*101 Dalmatians, Superman*) defending her choice to marry herself to a skeptical Joe Frank on his public radio program; she told him that every time she twirls the ring on her finger, she thinks about her commitment to be good to herself. Even *Sex and the City* used self-marriage as a passing bit of humor. When Carrie is feeling particularly downtrodden, she decides to marry herself and promptly registers for gifts (shoes, of course) at Manolo Blahnik.

Self-marriage does sound undeniably odd and probably is limited mostly to California performance artists (see stories on the following pages), but echoes of the choice to marry yourself are reverberating throughout our culture. Now that people are delaying marriage or choosing not to marry at all, more people are hungering for the coming-of-age ritual that marriage has become. For some people that's a bigger thirtieth or fortieth birthday party. For others it's the decision to buy a home by oneself. Small but growing numbers of single women are signing up for registries (formerly known as bridal registries) to signify that they, too, would like their share of flatware, crystal, and Crock-Pots. They've committed to a domestic life and a mortgage, if not a man.

The choice to marry yourself takes the coming-of-age ritual to a new level. It's not just about getting towels or diamond rings or attention. The common theme in most of the stories that I hear is a commitment to take care of oneself as one hopes or imagines that a lover would. Women also frame self-matrimony as a unique solution to the problem of women sacrificing their own needs in a relationship. Marry yourself first, they say, before marrying anyone else. I know two women who have wed themselves. Their stories follow.

Perhaps a future game show will ask not "Who Wants to Marry a Multimillionaire" but "Who Wants to Marry Themselves." Contestants will be judged on their self-care regimen: use of daily affirmations, living within their financial means (including savings), regular medical and dental check-ups, daily flossing, personal pampering, and getting proper sleep.

Aya de Leon

Current age: 35

Age of self-matrimony: 28

How she did it:

A Yoruba priest married

her, in a ritual that

included a lot of prayer

Where: On the beach

What she wore:

A simple dress

Aya de Leon, a San Francisco Bay Area performance poet, married herself and wrote about the experience for *Essence* magazine in June 1997. Now at work on a novel and a collection of essays, tentatively titled *How to Marry Yourself, and Other Scandalous Acts of Self-Love,* she explains: "As age thirty approaches, the pressures to get married are massive. But what's ironic is that for women, a lot of the time the experience is much more about the princess-for-the-day ritual. I noticed that women were obsessed with the cake, the dress, the pictures, looking beautiful. I decided at that time I didn't need the man to have the ritual. I was not dating anybody, but I felt that I needed to make a commitment to my life, to my creativity, my livelihood, my spirituality." Aya says that the wedding was a ritual, not a performance piece, and that having a community present was fundamental: "When you vow in public to do something, to make a commitment to take care of yourself, standing up in front of your community and doing that is life changing."

She continues, "The question I get all the time is, Will I have to divorce myself to marry someone else? No, not at all. My partner and I are preparing for our wedding now. I will probably wear some of the traditional bridal stuff because it is fun. I'm not taking his last name. I have told him when I get married I am unwilling to be referred to as his wife. Being a wife to someone has so much charge for me; historically that has meant working too hard, being underappreciated and exploited. It doesn't mean that people who take the title 'wife' have to be disempowered, but for me there's too much history. I will be my wife, and his partner."

By age thirty-seven, Remi Rubel had attended more than twenty weddings, ten bridal showers, and six baby showers. She wanted to be in a relationship, but the process of looking for a partner was not working well for her. She called herself a "magnet for relationships" but always felt like she was giving away too much. She decided to marry herself—in part to reverse this trend, and also to hush what she calls a harsh inner critic.

Remi's self-marriage was part of her graduate thesis project at the California College of Arts and Crafts. She threw herself a bridal shower and engagement party and sent herself on a honeymoon. By obtaining a ministership from the nondenominational Universal Life Church, she was able to marry herself at Mono Lake, an unusual, ancient lake at the foothills of the Sierra Nevada in California.

During the yearlong process of Remi's self-matrimony, she met and began dating a man named Ken. At first Remi resisted the relationship. But the quiet way in which Ken supported her project eventually won her over. "The fact that Ken supported my marriage to myself fully and came to love me throughout the process of marrying myself has been key to my falling in love with him. In addition, he was my wedding consultant, task partner, videographer, and photographer." Remi and Ken married exactly one year after Remi married herself, and Remi has since given birth to twin boys.

Remi credits at least part of her current emotional equilibrium to marrying herself first. "In past relationships with men, I often felt split in half by the compromises that I needed to make to keep the relationship intact. Since my self-marriage, I remain committed to myself first and don't splinter like I used to. Another thing I've noticed is that my harsh critic has toned down significantly since my two marriages. Being a bigamist has served me well."

How Remi did it (or how she tried):

First, Remi applied for and was granted ordination as a minister from the nondenominational Universal Life Church, which meant she could officiate at her own wedding. Obtaining a marriage license was more challenging. A clerk at the Alameda County Courthouse in Oakland rejected the application, claiming, "You have to be an unmarried man and an unmarried woman to legally marry." Remi planned to hold the ceremony in Mono County, so she tried again there—and met with surprisingly little resistance. However, two days after the wedding, a clerk called to say he didn't realize Remi was marrying herself. By marrying herself, Remi had violated three laws (the California Penal Code Section 360, Public Marriage VS 117, and California Family Code Section 420). Remi's marriage license was revoked and her money refunded.

Where Remi got married:

In a field, by a lake

Items on her wedding registry:

10 pc. combination wrench set

Leatherman original pocket tool

Sample vow:

"I will temper my desire for perfection while still maintaining the drive to excel. I look forward to a lifetime of curling up with you at night while we go to sleep, curling up so tight that we become one big bundle of bliss."

Honeymoon:

Spa retreat (where she ran into an old boyfriend)

14th District Assemblywoman
Dion Aroner
918 Parker Street, Suite A13
Berkeley, CA 94710

September 21, 1998

Dear Honorable Assemblywoman:

I am writing to you on behalf of the millions of single persons who have not yet been married and those who have been divorced and are not yet remarried. I believe that marriage to oneself should be made a prerequisite to marrying another person and that there should be legislation granting marriage licenses to individuals who marry themselves.

Currently, the law defines adulthood by setting a legal age to drink alcohol, smoke cigarettes, have sex, drive a car, and vote. Coming of age is also circumscribed by wedding another person and having children. Doesn't it make more sense to teach people how to commit to being responsible for themselves before making a life long commitment to their spouse or children? This seems particularly essential for women who are conditioned from childhood to take care of others before themselves.

If starting one's married life alone was legally supported, it would reinforce the message that wholeness must begin with the individual self.

If there is anything else I can do towards effecting legislative changes towards self-matrimony, please let me know.

As a newlywed recently married to myself, I eagerly await your response.

Yours sincerely,

Remi Rubel

Remi Rubel believes marrying yourself—like getting a blood test—should be a prerequisite for a legal ~~lice~~nse for a conventional marriage. She wrote ~~he~~r state representative, Dion Aroner, to suggest this idea.

~~Di~~on Louise Aroner ASSEMBLYWOMAN, FOURTEENTH DISTRICT
~~CALI~~FORNIA LEGISLATURE, STATE CAPITOL, SACRAMENTO, CA 95814 (916) 319-2014 FAX (916) 319-2114

CHAIR, ASSEMBLY HUMAN SERVICES
COMMITTEES:
JUDICIARY
REVENUE & TAXATION

SELECT COMMITTEES:
CALIFORNIA WOMEN
COASTAL PROTECTION

November 9, 1998

Remi Rubel

Dear Remi,

Thank you for your letter regarding marriage to oneself. As you mentioned in your letter, I believe being responsible for oneself before making a life long commitment to another person is important. Your suggestion is a unique way of approaching one's responsibility. I appreciate your input on this issue. Your idea is very interesting.

Thank you again for contacting my office and sharing your idea.

Sincerely,

Dion S. Aroner
Assemblywoman

Name: Matthue Roth

Age: 25

Hometown: Philadelphia, Pa.

Current town: San Francisco, Calif.

Favorite quirkyalone activities:
Dancing solo at rock shows.
Talking to strangers.
Dressing up.

Name: Jenny Makofsky

Age: 34

Hometown: Johnson City, N.Y.

Current town: Oakland, Calif.

Job: Writer/Performance Artist

Favorite Golden Girl: Tough to say: I'm going to have to go with Betty White, and the reason is that she used to be on *The Mary Tyler Moore Show*.

Favorite quirkyalone activities: Going to the library, making a zine, storytelling, hiking, signing up for focus groups, swimming, lurking in bookstores.

Personal QA motto: Es mejor estar solo que mal acompañado. Better unattached than unsuitably matched. (Mexican proverb)

Name: Walt Jacobs

Age: 35

Hometown: Atlanta, Ga.

Current town: Minneapolis, Minn.

Job: Assistant Professor
(sociology)

Length of time quirkyalone:
quirkyalone = life-long!
quirkytogether = 1.5 years

Relationship status: Quirkytogether
(engaged)

Personal QA motto: It's the process.
Being a QA means that you are
always reflecting on who you are
now in order to be something else.
The 'something else' varies from
QA to QA, but the thrill of the
process of inventing or discovering
something new about yourself is
more exciting than achieving it.

Name: LeVette Fuller

Age: 25

Hometown: Shreveport, La.

Current town: San Francisco, Calif.

Job: Barista/shopgirl

Length of time quirkyalone:
Three years

Relationship status: Single

Favorite Golden Girl: Rose

Personal QA motto: Don't settle,
don't settle. Being alone is far
more worthwhile.

"The real marriage of true minds

is for any two people to possess a sense

of humour or irony pitched in exactly the

same key, so that their joint glances at any

subject cross like interarching searchlights."

— Edith Wharton, *A Backward Glance*

chapter six
quirkytogether

One common misconception is that quirkyalones can't be in romantic relationships or that when they do enter into such blessed unions, their quirkyalone status goes on vacation or disappears. *Au contraire.* Never is the quirkyalone outlook more important than when we are romantically intertwined or, shall we say, when we are quirkytogether.

But what is quirkytogether? If we are to begin with a simple definition, let's first say this: QT takes the quirkyalone ethos of holding out for large-scale emotion and respecting the individual's need for space and puts those values into a relationship context. It typically involves a long-term romantic relationship in which one person is a quirkyalone and the other is accepting of that orientation, or one in which both partners are quirkyalone. In unusual cases, two nonquirkyalones may develop a quirkytogether lifestyle. They realize that they want an alternative, more open model of romantic relationships.

Quirkytogether is a flexible definition: therefore, there are many ways to be quirkytogether. Members of a quirkytogether couple bring in the elements of the quirkyalone ethic that are most important to them, whether it's a love of solitude, a need for separate

Quirkyalone Thought to Ponder: "Love consists in this, that two solitudes protect and touch and greet each other."—Rainer Maria Rilke, *Letters to a Young Poet*

space, the desire for continued passion and playfulness in the relationship (which might mean not seeing each other all the time or living in the same house or bedroom), or the need to maintain *über*-close friendships. People in a quirky-together partnership make up their own rules, challenging the tyranny of coupledom (the idea that everyone must be part of a pair at all times) and other business-as-usual notions about being in a relationship.

Most people assume that sleeping separately on occasion or all the time or living in separate apartments or houses indicates a problem in the relationship, a "fear of intimacy," or a festering resentment, but for quirkyalones, that's not necessarily the case. One quirkyalone woman—an artist, writer, and newlywed—describes the ideal she had before meeting her husband. "I never had an idealized person, but I did have an idealized image of how the relationship would be. Whenever I fantasized I basically thought this person would be awesome but they wouldn't be around all the time." She since has drawn an architectural sketch of her ideal quirky-together house. It includes several shared common areas, including kitchen and living room, but she and her husband have their own bedrooms.

At the core, quirkytogether values the idea of two fully formed human beings coming together for a partnership rather than a merging of souls—it's not the soul mate idea of finding the other half to complete you, but about finding a lively and dynamic partnership that still allows you to be fully yourself.

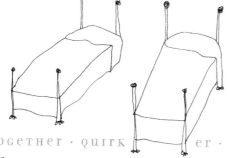

Quirkytogether Thought to Ponder:
Separate beds don't necessarily indicate a sexless *Ozzie and Harriet*–style relationship.

Moreover, a quirkytogether relationship does not ask you to give up your past, to jettison everything you have learned during years of single, sexual, autonomous living. Life before the "relationship" was not just a prologue to the "real thing." All of life is the real thing. Let's face it: when you have spent years in a sin-

Atlantic Beach, North Carolina is for *Lovers Quirkytogethers*

gular state, there will be compromise and adjustment moving into a coupled mode, but you're not about to trade in your entire being for the new relationship. If you love eating peas out of a can (secret single behavior #1) or going on vacations with your friends, those activities will need to be maintained.

In some essential ways, some quirkyalones in relationships still feel like they are single and that this is not a sign of the relationship's demise but a frank recognition of the ultimate human condition (in all its good and bad ways). Aimee Mann, former lead singer of Til Tuesday, who first rode to fame in the eighties with a song, "Voices Carry," that cautioned against being silent in a relationship, is a good pop culture example of someone with this point of view. She married her soul mate in singer Michael Penn in 1998, but on a promotional Web site she explains that a lot of the songs on her 2000 album *Bachelor No. 2* "are about being single, regardless of being married or not." She also sounds pretty quirkytogether in this statement: "My relationship with Michael is so unique that there are ways in which I don't really feel like I'm having a relationship, because I've defined 'relationship' as being this sort of unwieldy, nightmarish thing."

The archetypal image of quirkytogethers: two people sitting on the couch reading with their feet intertwined; two solitudes that protect each other and also join together.

FROM UNTETHERED TO TETHERED

Of course, the transition from quirkyalone to quirkytogether is not always alto-gether smooth. (And even when you do get there, it's rarely nirvana. All those nonquirkyalones are basically right: even the best relationships do take work.) The transition can take a while, since we take marriages and even boyfriend-girlfriend relationships seriously. It can even take a quirkyalone a long time to feel comfortable with the terms *boyfriend* or *girlfriend*.

And then there's the rocky transition from fantasy to reality.

The extended daydreaming one has in R.O. as a single quirkyalone about what a relationship will be like is ultimately all about me, me, me: someone gets all

---

QUIRKYTOGETHERS DO:
- Think critically about the institution of marriage
- Endeavor to plan and pay for their own weddings (if they plan on tying the knot)
- Accept that they are distinct individuals—not always the plural "we"
- Maintain an open mind about how relationships can work
- Support partners having strong friendships outside of "the relationship"
- Share their "hopes and dreams" but also encourage each other to follow their individual aspirations

QUIRKYTOGETHERS DON'T:
- Wear matching sweaters
- Joke about having to escape each other, e.g., the "old ball and chain"
- Throw couples-only dinner parties
- Clone each other's interests; your new boyfriend golfs, so you become a golfer. QAs don't become a new person with each relationship.
- Get mad when one partner wants to stay home and the other wants to go out; it's okay to leave the house as an individual
- Suffer a fundamental identity crisis when and if they break up (what am I going to do with myself now?)
- Send out holiday cards with a Sears portrait of themselves on the cover

> "Perkytogether": The quirkyalone's natural opposite.
> While there are many people whom quirkyalones can respectfully
> recognize as not sharing their worldview, perkytogethers impose
> coupledom on everyone. They are the tyranny of coupledom.

these things about you, and you will do all the activities together that you have dreamed about. In fantasyland, you meet someone, and you just "know" that you are meant to be together. You don't have to get to know someone gradually and be vulnerable in the process by letting that person know what you need and require in a relationship. Obviously a relationship involves two people; it's not a dictatorship willed into life from imagination. It can be strange to trade this imaginary person (the one who fits your list of hoped-for qualities in a mate, the one that matches your personal ad) for a real person. When you have constructed your romantic expectations as though every day is Christmas Eve, it might be hard to accept that it is finally Christmas.

A quirkyalone in a relationship has to learn all the lessons that everyone else has to learn. The number one lesson is astonishingly simple but still hard to assimilate. It's the very basic ontological idea that the partner is not you. As the writer Iris Murdoch so wisely put it, "Love is the extremely difficult realization that someone other than oneself is real."

Not only does an intimate, long-term romantic relationship not provide permanent bliss, it also can lead to conflict, compromise, and even having to deal with very mundane matters of divergent attitudes toward money, laundry, cleanliness, paying bills, and dealing with in-laws. That can be a hard lesson for anyone to accept—and even harder for quirkyalones, who are used to doing their own thing their own way. Also, what happened to our romantic visions? They have been subsumed in the day-to-day "work" of being in a relationship.

But of course a relationship should not be all work. If it is, that's probably a bad sign. Quirkyalones are still romantics, after all. Quirkytogether is aligned with the upper-case definition of *Romantic*—not weddings that dazzle guests, matching bathrobes, and constant togetherness, but small, personalized, individual gestures. The small moments of being in love at the beginning of a relationship: you and your new beloved have a conversation about Slim Jims, so you drop off a bouquet of Slim Jims at the door. Later on, these moments can be as simple as helping each other to make a pros-and-cons list late into the night about whether to stay at or leave a job, collaborating on a collage, or having a pillow fight. Your partner is a close friend. Amazingly enough, however, you are also attracted to each other, and you enjoy the bonus of physical intimacy.

QUIRKYALONES AND MARRIAGE: IS IT POSSIBLE?

What about quirkyalones and marriage? Is it possible? Of course. Quirkyalones are unique people, but we don't live in a paranormal universe. As you will read in this chapter, many of the quirkyalones who are quoted have taken the plunge into holy matrimony. But not everyone feels the need to tie the knot or display a diamond ring. Some quirkyalones may even feel repulsed by the trappings of traditional marriage, an institution rooted in the idea of women as property that devalues friendship and elevates the sexual or romantic relationship above all else. If quirkyalones are not interested in dating for the sake of dating, they are definitely not interested in getting married for the sake of being wed.

If quirkyalones do marry, often it's later in life. And here is the good news: there is something to be said for waiting. Sociologist Tim Heaton of Brigham Young University set out to investigate the decline of the divorce rate during the last decade. His repeated statistical tests isolate one key variable responsible for more

"It is a strange transition to be with someone else. When you are on your own, you have so much time to yourself. You are like your own therapist; you start to understand yourself. Being with someone on a daily basis, there can be confrontations and conflict; you have to see yourself as perceived by someone else and make a lot of adjustments. You have to sort it out and bring the relationship-mind up to speed."

—Margo, quirkytogether/quirkyalone (quirkytogether for the first time in five years)

stable marital unions: age at marriage. In a nutshell, marriages have been more stable in recent years simply because the average American bride and groom have been slower to reach the altar.

If we do marry, most female quirkyalones do not want to relinquish their last names. Many of us feel more comfortable with the term *partner* than *wife*. Given the cultural legacy of marriage as an institution, "partner" sets a more egalitarian tone; with all the expectations about how a "wife" is supposed to behave, it's much easier to feel like a "bad wife" than a "bad partner."

Another aspect of quirkytogether may be a realism about relationships and an appreciation for various relationships in our lives, ones that don't necessarily need to be lifelong or follow the typical Rockwellian ideal of growing old together, sitting on a veranda, sipping lemonade. For some, there's nothing wrong with the idea of having various soul mates or partners over the course of a lifetime.

Further Reading for Quirkyalones Embarking on Relationships

Happy All The Time: Laurie Colwin's charming 1978 novel of manners is one of the best fictional depictions of the sometimes-bumpy psychological transition from QA to QA/QT. (Quirkyalones do sometimes resist romantic relationships, out of fear of vulnerability, losing their "edge" or their identities as unattached.) In *Happy All The Time*, four idiosyncratic bourgeois New Yorkers fall in love. During a decade when women were still considered primarily wives rather than workers, the two female characters resist traditional views about romantic relationships and force their men to respect boundaries and separate space. Intimidatingly smart linguist Misty Berkovitz (a prickly cynic with a deceptively feminine name) is the most obvious quirkyalone. At least two descriptions of Misty must be shared—they could not be more aligned with the quirkyalone aesthetic: "She had always known that her appeal was not general. The general run of man did not want someone as quirky as she was. . . . [S]he was a special case of one sort or another. Only another special case might truly love her and since those were rare, and Misty was not a compromiser, it was clear to her that she would probably float through life alone." In another scene, she expresses the archetypal quirkyalone attitude toward dating as a way of life: "She was not and had never been interested in social life as it was commonly conducted. She did not wish to be taken out for dinner or to have a beau. She was interested in ultimates . . . like passion and honor."

William and Alice, both in their fifties, are two quirkyalones in a couple who are very much in love and have been together for several years. But they don't necessarily see their relationship as lasting in the same way forever. Detailed and open communication about their commitment to each other is, however, a priority. William explains: "We are both very open to the possibility that at some point one or both of us might want to move on. We decided to live together for a year to see how it works and then make an assessment. One clear option is that I would move back to my house if it doesn't work. We have said that every year we will take some time reviewing and making decisions about our relationship, to see if we want to renew our vows, change them, or move on. It's not in our minds that this relationship has to go on forever, but it can go on in a wonderful way and we will still be friends. I think that's a big difference in terms of being a quirky couple. I feel very fortunate to be where I am right now, but it took me fifty years to get here."

Name: Steve Larosiliere

Age: 28

Hometown: Brooklyn, N.Y.

Current town: Brooklyn, N.Y.

Job: Recruitment Manager, Mentoring USA

Length of time quirkyalone: Six years

Relationship status: Quirkytogether

Favorite Golden Girl: Blanche

Favorite quirkyalone activities: Reading, being cozy

Mixed-status couples. Or, can a quirkyalone
be in a relationship with a nonquirkyalone?

One of the most perplexing questions is whether quirkyalones need to be with other quirkyalones or whether they work best with those who are distinctly not. We might think that a quirkyalone with another quirkyalone is ideal. Both partners would understand the need for separate space and time; with all that time apart, there would still be the ability to idealize the beloved, to keep the flame alive in a long-term relationship. It could be so intense, so passionate, so meaningful, almost like Cathy and Heathcliff from *Wuthering Heights:* two souls destined to be together. "I love him, and that, not because he is handsome, Nelly, but because he's more myself than I am. Whatever our souls are made of, his and mine are the same, and Linton's is as different as a moonbeam from lightning, or frost from fire."

Then again, a double-quirkyalone couple might be challenging. Quirkyalones are often quite introspective. It might be better to partner with someone who can take you out of your head to live in the here and now. Nonquirkyalones also may have a grounding and consistency that quirkyalones lack, the ability to see through the rough spots of a relationship, to take the long view and not head for the border as soon as there's a problem. Let's face it: a lot of QAs are not very good at making the first move. When two quirkyalones meet, the earth may quake. But they also might repel each other with mutual shyness and inertia.

Curious about the perspectives of some of my coupled comrades, I asked various QAs for their perspectives. Their insights follow.

Chelsea expressed her feelings about being married to a nonquirkyalone: "My husband is the opposite of a quirkyalone. He hates being alone, hates it. That is an interesting combination. I think you have to be careful; one gets very used to being alone and having space and the time for things to absorb. We're so overstimulated every day, and there is something about solitude that allows your thoughts to take shape; if you are in constant company there is a feeling for me of never settling internally. There needs to be some time and space. If people are willing to be malleable, you can change your habits and adapt. It's very human to compromise."

Jennifer, married to a nonquirkyalone, has come to appreciate the value of their differences: "I used to imagine I would be with someone like me, but if I were, we might drive each other crazy. I can really overanalyze everything, withdraw and mull in unhealthy ways. That is not his style. He is not shallow, but he doesn't feel the weight of life to the degree I sometimes do. I think about the future constantly; he lives in the moment. That's great for me. He takes me out of myself. He is unquestionably quirky. I think I definitely need quirky. I don't recommend that a quirkyalone be with a nonquirky person; that is a recipe for disaster."

Beth, married to another quirkyalone, says she could *only* be married to another quirkyalone: "The advantages are that there's low stress in terms of feeling like you need to be 'on' for the other person all the time. Since quirkyalones choose to spend a goodly time apart, the time spent together is often 'quality,' even if it's something as mundane as doing the dishes.

"Finances can be kept separate without feeling like you are betraying a societal standard: we keep separate checking accounts, separate closets. He's an accountant who can't for the life of him balance his own checkbook. I flunked math and can balance my accounts to the penny. It would be too much hassle to maintain finances together—when he forgets to tell me about the forty dollars he took out for groceries and we start bouncing checks. Quirkyalones prefer to have control of their happiness; to me that includes a balanced checkbook!

"Separate vacations—definitely!—without feeling like your partner will feel abandoned."

Dual-Dwelling Duos: A term coined by Judye Hess and Padma Catell in the *Journal of Couples' Therapy* to describe an alternative for long-term relationships, in which "each member of the couple chooses to retain their own separate domicile while still being in a committed, monogamous, and loving relationship." These two therapists write, if "there were more options available for long-term relationships, and these options were considered healthy and desirable, some people could be spared the trauma of divorce or breakup of their relationships." On the downside, "By living separately, the partners might miss some of the shared creativity of building a home together. They may get less recognition from society for the value or seriousness of their relationship, and they will have less of an opportunity to create or try to replicate their original family closeness." The advantages are an ability "to retain the excitement and aliveness that comes with the continued feelings of longing for their beloved. . . . DDDs [also] do not have to constantly deal with the differences in their standards of neatness, tastes in music, desired amount of social contact, among many others. The partners who do not live together can come together out of choice and desire, rather than because they share the same space and have no other options."

William Poy Lee, living with another quirkyalone, on the emotional nuances of their situation: "When you have intentional long periods of time alone and you are really going into your own thoughts, as much as you love each other, the transition [back together] can be a little rough. One thing I noticed was that after spending some time apart we would look at each other and go, Who is this person? It's like meeting someone you don't quite know because you have been so into your alone space until that moment. After a few hours you are able to be together in a way that reflects all the past love and time, and that alone-space person you were then looks like a stranger. We decided to move in together in part because of the roughness of these transitions.

"In the natural flow of being a quirkycouple, we help each other protect our own space. When we moved in together, we defined our space, her space, my space. Within the house we are trying to replicate the kind of choice we had [as singles] to have alone space. Where I work is my cave. She has a little casita, a little cottage, and then the kitchen, dining room, and living room are common. We sleep together, but if one of us wanted to be alone, we just say so, we don't get into this 'Oh, you don't love me.' If she says, 'I feel like sleeping alone,' that's fine. We have two different beds. There is nothing we need to argue about or explain. It has never happened that either of us wanted to sleep alone for an extended period of time. If that happened there would need to be a discussion."

QUIRKYALONES AND LONG-DISTANCE RELATIONSHIPS:
Quirkytogether and Quirkyapart

One question that some single quirkyalones may ask themselves: Why is it that we often fall for people who live in other cities? Maybe it really is because all the attractive people live elsewhere—in which case no one is really attractive once you get to know them. That's a little bleak. Or, to dig a little deeper, maybe it's because we open ourselves up to the possibility of love more often when we step out of our everyday routines. We might be stuck in certain social grooves at home, eyes averted from strangers we pass on the street. In a new city we meet new friends of friends—and how intriguing they may seem. Or maybe the bias toward love with people in other cities is based on fear: love *has* to conquer all because it could be *years* before we find someone else who even comes close again. Or maybe, just maybe, long-distance relationships make a certain sense to us, at least at certain points in our lives, when we may want romance, sex, and emotional intimacy but we're not entirely convinced that we want a quotidian relationship—someone who is always around and may occupy time and space we realistically need to reserve for ourselves. A far-flung alliance can be intense and intimate but still allow for tons of free time, space, and room. The long-distance challenge supports the idea that the love is so special and unique that it has to be nurtured no matter what the obstacles. It can also be sexy. That which is difficult, which is complicated and unconventional, often can be. There are disadvantages, of course. With far-flung love, you miss out on massages, home-cooked dinners, the everyday love and support of a real, physical body. If you are putting work in the relationship, you might not feel like you are getting a great return—because, guess what, the person is not there! Basically, for the quirkyalone, the bottom line is this: for most people there are only cons associated with long-distance relationships. For us, there are pros and cons.

premiere issue

$3.00

To-Do List

a magazine of meaningful minutiae

To-Do List P.O. Box 40128, SF, CA 94140

the quirkyalone,

the depths of Silicon Valley, adulthood revisited, flossing, dated then hated, airborne conversation, reasons to live. **lists!**

100

I Fell in Love with a quirkyalone

by Kevin Bundy

I'm not one to go for theories about emergent personality types. There's something smelling of snake oil in self-help books that divide society into easy categories, as if the truly endless possibilities of human character could be squeezed into a couple of boxes labeled "Venus" and "Mars." But I have to admit that I've fallen in love with a quirkyalone.

My parents may have belonged to the last generation for which getting together defined the meaning of life, and failing to stay together marked its profoundest disillusionment. Yet the allure of the so-called relationship remains strong. I've spent most of my adolescent and adult life trying desperately not to be alone, seeking the addictive bliss of new love, holding on to it for a while, and pretending nothing is amiss while it stales and sours. I've been married and divorced, had my heart broken and broken another's heart in turn.

Looking back, at times I wish I'd had the strength to be a quirkyalone.

We're imprinted, like so many half-finished circuit boards, with those Disneyesque happy endings: girl meets boy, animated sparks fly, the slipper fits, and the credits roll. But once we're thus smitten, we don't know what to do—the Disney movie ends, conveniently, before the relationship begins. So we plug along, not quite in tandem, hoping somehow that those initial animated sparks will light our way through confining ruts, slow disillusionments, and eventual darkness ahead. We can spend years with one another, yet never really be together.

Six months or so ago I fell in love with a quirkyalone, and thankfully, she won't let us get away with just "being together." Her standards are higher. She likes engagement, not just conversation; exuberance, not just interest. Quirkyalones seem more solid than the rest of us, preferring the thoughtful quiet of solitude to a depthless togetherness. I've realized I'm not essential to her happiness. I occasionally serve as an obstacle. Her world doesn't revolve around me.

That kind of revelation can be a real blow to even the most sensitive, progressive fragile male ego.

On the other hand, falling in love with a quirkyalone seems to pose a worthwhile challenge, an opportunity to get over some of the mythology that hinders romantic miracles and to set to work on the far tougher task of actually creating some. I think quirkyalones, paradoxically, are comfortable being alone precisely because they believe very strongly in the possibility of profound human connection, of friendships that define lifetimes, of love that really shakes the world. They also know that such miracles are rare, that passing fancies seldom blossom into soulful interests, and that anything short of perfect just might not be worth the effort.

I do get frustrated. I want her to cut me some slack, to let me off the hook sometimes, to pass over the occasional imperfect conversation without an hour of scrupulous analysis. Lazy self-absorption still appeals to me every now and then. Yet I know that the initial ease of an unexamined relationship soon turns inside out. I'm also finally overcoming some bad habits, listening more actively, speaking more honestly, and finding out that she's more interesting than I ever would have discovered.

I don't know if it's going to "work out" between us. I'm not sure what that means anymore, though the Disney films of my childhood still whisper "happily ever after" in my ear. I fear that if I don't work as hard as she does, she'll retreat to the solid comfort of her quirkyaloneness, and I'll be left alone without the quirks, or the confidence, to get by. But that's precisely the point. We have to develop the patience and self-knowledge as individuals to insist on the kind of love that we want, or we're never going to find it, no matter how many relationships we set alight and watch burn out. She's setting a good example for me, and if we ultimately can't make the earth quake, I think I'm going to try going it (quirky)alone for a while. Who knows, I just might be tough enough.

Kevin Bundy does outreach and advocacy for a grassroots environmental organization in northern California. He has sworn off all Disney movies.

> falling in love with a quirkyalone seems to pose a worthwhile challenge, an opportunity to get over some of the mythology that hinders romantic miracles . . . and work on actually creating some.

Reprinted from To-Do List, *premiere issue*

More quirkytogether thoughts to ponder

A leading male voice in the quirkyalone movement, Andrew Boyd read the following excerpt, "Loving the Wrong Person," from his book, *Daily Afflictions: The Agony of Being Connected to Everything in the Universe*, at the New York celebration of IQD-2003. At the end of his reading, Andrew led the crowd in chanting the mantra that concludes this piece.

LOVING THE WRONG PERSON

"Let our scars fall in love."—Galway Kinnell

We're all seeking that special person who is right for us. But if you've been through enough relationships, you begin to suspect there's no right person, just different flavors of wrong. Why is this? Because you yourself are wrong in some way, and you seek out partners who are wrong in some complementary way. But it takes a lot of living to grow fully into your own wrongness. And it isn't until you finally run up against your deepest demons, your unsolvable problems—the ones that make you truly who you are—that you're ready to find a lifelong mate. Only then do you finally know what you're looking for. You're looking for the wrong person. But not just any wrong person: the right wrong person—someone you lovingly gaze upon and think, "This is the problem I want to have."

I will find that special person who is wrong for me in just the right way.

Reprinted with permission from *Daily Afflictions* by Andrew Boyd, published by W. W. Norton, www.dailyafflictions.com

QAs SAY: LIVE FREE OR DIE

Name: Carolyn Jacobs

Age: 27

Hometown: Boston, Mass.

Current town: San Francisco, Calif.

Relationship status: Currently in a really healthy relationship, the kind I wasn't sure existed. Working to maintain my quirkyalone, quirkytogether, and quirkyslut identities all at once. Is this possible??

Favorite quirkyalone activities: Hanging with the ladies, yoga, art projects, and honking the horn at CBs (cute boys) around town

Personal QA motto: Closest thing I can think of is "Live free or die." Living independently, creatively, passionately, honestly, without letting fear or the tyranny of coupledom take over.

Name: Nicola Warwick

Age: 39

Hometown: Manchester, U.K.

Current town: Manchester, U.K.

Job: Business Services Manager
for U.K. Telco

Length of time quirkyalone: Most
of my adult life but especially in
my thirties. Single this time
round since I was thirty-one.

Favorite quirkyalone activities:
Snap-happy photography,
browsing in bookshops, writing
in cafés, kickboxing, writing
long letters, Web design

Personal QA motto: All or
nothing. I'm not good at settling for second best. I'd rather
be single than with the wrong
man. I'd rather have nothing
than all the wrong things. I'd
rather go the whole hog than
do things half-heartedly.

Name: Karen Harrison

Age: 57

Hometown: Boulder, Colo.

Current town: Boulder, Colo.

Job: Teacher and Student

Length of time quirkyalone:
Seventeen years as quirkyalone;
fifty-seven years in support of
quirkyalones

Relationship status: Divorced for
longer than I was married

Favorite Golden Girl: Katharine
Hepburn

Favorite quirkyalone activities:
Hiking, reading, reacting to news,
mulling over issues

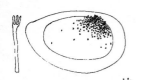

Friendship:
For quirkyalones,
it's more than
a side dish.

chapter seven
best friends 4-eva

I don't think I am unusual among quirkyalones when I say that friendship has always come more naturally to me than romantic love. I may not have had romantic relationships always, but I have always had friends—best friends, intense friends, casual friends, fast friends—and felt passionately devoted to many of them. When people ask me about my relationship history, I can tell them about all my botched romances and crazy affairs. Good stories all, and probably better as narrative than as actual experience, but if I am really to tell someone the story of my life, it is a story of friendships. From third grade on, my friends have been the people with whom I have probed the questions of the universe: Do you believe in God? What should I do with my life? How do you feel about oral sex? Where did you get those pants, and what size are they?

Now that I am an adult, friendship is no less important to me than it was in elementary school. Last night I slept over at my friend Sara's apartment. We shared her bed and talked until past 1 A.M. We don't kiss. We don't have sex. It's not the nature of our relationship. But we share deep thoughts with each other and fight ironically about who gets to share which deep thoughts first. We laugh hysterically. We know each others' neuroses as if they were our own. We don't call each other life partners, though we are

Quirkyalone Thought to Ponder: "Some people go to priests; others to poetry; I to my friends."—Virginia Woolf

probably closer to life partners than anyone else in our lives. But we have other life partners too. That is the beauty of friendship: it's intimate, but it's not exclusive.

Friendship is truly the missing link for quirkyalones. So many of us started out in adulthood looking for "the one." What we find along the way is something more diffuse, perhaps more rich: "the two," "the three," or "the four." Why have one soul mate when you can have many? I can always tell I may be talking to another quirkyalone when conversational references involve friends as frequently as they do romantic partners. Rather than just, "My boyfriend last summer" or "The girl I was dating," they say, "My friends and I often talk about" or "My friend and I took a road trip."

The obvious reason for our focus on friendship is that we have spent significant amounts of time outside of a relationship, so we look for and cultivate significant emotional bonds with platonic friends. Mitch Goldman, a very friend-centric quirkyalone, explains, "Close friends can provide a lot of what a romantic relationship provides. There's always someone to hang out with and, on an emotional level, a person you can confide in. Friendships also have characteristics that romantic relationships often don't. A lot of my friends can by very crude. They are comfortable with any flaws I may have. In relationships I have been in, there has always been a little holding back—you want to put forth your best side." Lindsey Moreland agrees: "When you are single so long, your friends take on that primary support position. I see a lot of people going into their own world when they

Alison, a quirkyalone in her thirties: "My big fear is growing old alone. I think about it all the time. But I look at how people relate when they are older. My mom's friend is an interesting example. Her good friend got divorced five or six years ago and was later diagnosed with cancer. What's amazing is the support she has had from her friends. Her friends have formed a support group and take turns coming over. Her ex-husband has nothing to do with it. It's her friends who are really there."

According to celebratefriendship.org, a dictionary in 1755 defined friendship as "the highest degree of intimacy."

couple up. I can see the temptation of that—this person is your lover, your friend, your support system—but I don't think it works that way."

We value our friendships not just because they are relationship substitutes, but because they have virtues that relationships do not.

Because there is no one road map for friendships, they are allowed breathing room to develop organically over time. Close friendships can have a level of effortlessness, naturalness, and grace that all but the very best romantic relationships lack. The best times are when we lounge on a friend's bed like walruses, talking about whatever happens to come to mind. We don't have to think about what we are saying; whatever comes out of our mouths is okay—no fears, no censorship, you can be utterly yourself. Women's magazines give readers tips on how to be "superclose" with a guy. That supercloseness is often already there in many friendships. Friends understand each other; if they had to work at understanding each other, they wouldn't be friends.

GROWING UP: ARE THE DAYS OF SLUMBER PARTIES OVER?

When we are children, it's normal to value our friends so much. We pledge our commitment through friendship bracelets and by becoming blood sisters and brothers. As adults, we learn that a romantic and sexual relationship is supposed to provide primary companionship, and though friendships are important, they become the side dish.

Denise, a quirkyalone in her early forties, talks about her "gay husband" Keith: "We've been friends for about twelve years. We hang about three nights a week. Sometimes we go to gallery openings or dancing, but mainly we hang out and watch television. One day I just used the term gay husband because we are like an old married couple. We don't have sex; we never did. We just lounge around watching movies. He brings over fashion magazines when he is finished reading them, and he gives me lots of good fashion advice. He'll be really honest about the way things look. We get into fights—'Oh, honey,' he says, 'that's not working on you.' We argue and yell at each other. He calls us Mr. and Mrs. Lockhorn. He runs to the corner store for snacks, desserts, to get me a Sunday paper or a half gallon of milk. He doesn't fix things, but he washes dishes and takes out the trash and recycling. Sometimes I cook for him. I bring a sense of stability for him. I was telling this woman about him; she said we could all use a gay husband. But it doesn't have to be a gay man. If my friend Frances who lives in New York lived here, I would be hanging out with her all the time too. She would be my straight wife."

Everyone needs to have friends, but our culture doesn't position them as the central ingredient of a happy life. There are no love songs on the radio devoted to friendship. There are no public ceremonies devoted to friends. No one wonders where a friend-ship is going. No one asks if friends are "getting serious."

And yet in the twenty-first century it is almost impossible to overemphasize the importance of platonic friendship. Now that most people spend long periods of time outside the marital bond, with marriages happening later and divorce more common, these nonsexual bonds are more vital for all of us. Situation comedies in the 1980s took the family as their natural backdrop (*The Cosby Show, Family Ties, Who's the Boss?*). Now, if the most popular shows are not called *Friends*, they are about friends: *Seinfeld, Will and Grace, Ally McBeal, Sex and the City.* In 2002 Ethan Watters published an essay in the *New York Times Magazine* giving a name and a definition to these relationships and released a book on the same topic in 2003. Where other social commentators saw a commitment-phobic generation in the thirteen million "never-marrieds" between the ages of twenty-five and thirty-nine, Watters saw a new type of community: the urban tribe, groups of friends that mark the passage of time with celebrations, travel, moving one another's furniture, and cheering each other on at sporting events and open-mike nights. With the support of the urban tribe, he writes, "Single life in the city is no longer a phase that need be concluded quickly. With little fanfare, we've added a developmental stage to adulthood that comes before marriage—the tribe years."

Of course, success in the realm of friendship can get in the

"I don't think quirkyalones get into romantic relationships with their friends very often. It's a sacred space. If we go out, we might have to break up. I don't want to break up."
—Margot, quirkyalone

"Thanksgiving is the classic coming out for a mate, so no one could understand it. How could I bring home a female and not be dating?"
—Mitch, twentysomething quirkyalone

way of dating. Being so satisfied with your friends can make it awfully hard to sit through an awkward date. Anne McLaughlin, forty-two, a writer and activist from Idaho, explains, "Perhaps my friendships keep me so satisfied, I don't need to seek very hard for companionship."

Friendship does not provide everything. It doesn't provide sex or an ultimate emotional merging. The nature of friendship is to embrace intimacy while remaining separate. We may expect a lot of our friends, but we don't expect them to solve all our problems or make us emotionally complete. And maybe that's a good thing. In her antimarriage screed, *Here Comes the Bride: Women, Weddings, and the Marriage Mystique*, Jaclyn Geller makes the point that the qualities of friendship would be good ones to consider for romantic love: "Those who wonder what model would replace wedlock if the institution of marriage fell away fail to recognize that the model already exists. The paradigm is platonic friendship, unfettered by social institutions . . . untainted by the legacy of gender inequity. The forces that guide successful friendships are privacy, uniqueness, the acceptance of other relationships, individuality, autonomy, and open-endedness. If these qualities could guide amorous relationships . . . such depressurized unions would probably be much happier."

FEAR OF FRIENDSHIP-ABANDONMENT

But is basing your life on your friendships the best way to live beyond your twenties and thirties? Friendship, like an amorous relationship, takes time to maintain, and in their middle years, inevitably, people need to pour energy and

famous friends

WES ANDERSON AND OWEN WILSON

THE *Seinfeld* GANG

THE WOMEN OF *Sex and the City*

WILL AND GRACE

D. H. LAWRENCE AND HILDA DOOLITTLE (H.D.)

THE BEATS

JAMES WATSON AND FRANCIS CRICK (discoverers of the structure of DNA)

THELMA AND LOUISE

NICOLE KIDMAN AND NAOMI WATTS

MARY AND RHODA

SCULLY AND MULDER

JIM AND HUCK FINN

PENN AND TELLER

ELIZABETH CADY STANTON AND SUSAN B. ANTHONY

JO MARCH AND LAURIE (from *Little Women*)

(and Laverne and Shirley, of course!)

Danielle, quirkytogether in her late twenties, says this of her twin sister, Julie: "I always remember this conversation with my grandmother. My Nana asked Julie, 'Who is your best friend?' Of course Julie said 'Danielle.' Nana said, 'No, you're married now.' She went into this big lecture about how we need to be loyal to our husbands first and no longer call each other best friends. I thought about it a lot afterward. I started to wonder if emotionally that might be true. Now that Julie's married, her best friend has to be Jeff. Julie might start a new family, and that would be the most important thing. A month or so later Julie and I took a road trip. We were having a heart-to-heart talk. She told me, 'I just wanted to tell you that when Nana said to me that Jeff should be my best friend, I didn't believe that for one second. You are my best friend.'"

time into their homes, their spouses, and their children. Whether we are quirkyalone or not, we all experience tremendous anxiety and fear of abandonment when our siblings and friends pair up. The social and economic system is set up for couples. Quirkyalones can feel increasingly close to loneliness (not blessed solitude) when all their friends are going the route of Noah's Ark. If you're the last quirkyalone standing—or rather, the last nonQT quirkyalone standing—no matter how brave and proud and solid, you will still think in those moments just before dawn or at a friend's wedding, "Wait, have I been fooling myself?"

The movie *Walking and Talking* is a cult favorite because it addresses this anxiety head-on. The film opens with two young best friends lying on a bed looking at *The Joy of Sex.* They regard the pictures with awe and disgust. "Look, he's grabbing her boobs!" "Gross!" The next scene jumps twenty years ahead, with the same two women, Amelia (Catherine Keener) and Laura (Anne Heche), in their early thirties. Laura has recently moved out of their shared apartment and in with her boyfriend. The night she gets engaged, she goes to sleep with a new anxiety: "Oh my God, how am I going to tell Amelia?" When Amelia does find out she tries to act happy, but the truth comes out when she sees her therapist: "My best friend's getting married, that's probably what's making me sick." With lines like these, the movie is probably the most astonishingly real depiction of an intense female friendship in cinema or in print.

A mainstream film reviewer might name these fears jealousy. But that's not really what's going on at the heart of the film. More than jealousy, what propels *Walking and Talking* is a fear of abandonment. In their most dramatic fight scene, Amelia lays it on the line: "When something happens in my life, good or bad, I tell you. I need you. Now when something happens in your life, you tell Frank." Laura tries to explain that yes, she does have Frank, but she still needs her, that marriage will change her life but it does not exempt her from loneliness.

If you have never gone through such an intense transition with a friend, the scene could seem melodramatic. But for me—and probably most (female) quirkyalones—it is riveting. The characters are speaking lines that so many of us thought but never said when our friends embarked on romantic relationships because we are supposed to play it cool. We're not supposed to have the same degree of need and passion in our friendships as we do in relationships. We smother the feeling because it's not socially acceptable. But friendship is not casual for quirkyalones. It *can* be casual, but it can also be incredibly important, raw, and real.

Part of the problem is that we lack the rituals to value our friendships and language to describe them. (Maybe if there were an adult equivalent to our best-friend rituals of youth—becoming blood sisters and brothers or wearing friendship bracelets—we wouldn't worry about being displaced when our friends start romantic relationships. See "Boston Marriages and other Friendship Rites," on page 115, for examples of how other societies use ceremonies to recognize important friends.) One thing I have noticed is that we often use humor to talk about our friendships. My friend Ali lives with a Kate. They joke about setting up a household with kids à la *Kate and Allie,* the 1980s television show about

Danielle continues, "It makes me think that marriage and finding that romantic partner—it's not the same anymore. My Nana didn't have a job, all of her friends were married, they all stayed home. Now that women's roles are changing and we are workers, writers, mothers, divorced, or lesbians, friends do become more important than they used to be. Our lives are even more diverse than men's are because of kids and motherhood. We are no longer in that era that our husbands are our best friends and that's it. It cannot be emphasized too much that now, more than ever—and especially for women—having a friend is as important as anything."

two single mothers who live together. Another friend and I joke about buying a house together in our hometown. These statements are tentative—in part, for fear that either of us will take the proposal seriously. Ultimately, I think some of us are afraid to admit that we really might like to shack up with a friend. It would be seen as pathetic, an inferior arrangement to living with a romantic partner—even though it by no means would preclude other relationships.

Recently I met one quirkyalone who seems to have worked around this dilemma to create a best-of-both-worlds scenario, with allegiance to both romantic and platonic love. Amy Rathbone is an artist whom I asked to create illustrations for this book. While we were meeting to discuss her drawings (one of which was intended to illustrate the importance of friendship for quirkyalones), Amy mentioned that she and her best friend and roommate, Jody, are planning to throw a tenth-anniversary party to celebrate their friendship. They will register for gifts at the ninety-nine-cent store. "It's a joke party," she explains, "but realistically it's a way for us to acknowledge the love that we have for each other."

Jody and Amy met in Prague ten years ago when Jody was visiting a boyfriend and Amy was living there working on an art installation. Over time they exchanged many letters ("almost like love letters," Amy says). Jody moved to San Francisco, and Amy decided to go to school there as well. Amy says, "I remember coming to visit the school before moving here. She had planned a whole day, meeting her friends and taking me to the beach. It felt kind of like dating, but we're not lesbians. We moved in together and have lived together for six and a half years. She has become like my sister. My friendship with her is incredibly encouraging. I remember growing up there was a lot of talk about jealousy between friends; it's not that way between us. We haven't made a vocal commitment that we will be together for the rest of our lives, but it really does feel like a marriage on some level."

Amy continues, "In terms of quirkyalone, we talk a lot about the idea of moving out and moving in with a male partner. We both have boyfriends, and it's something we struggle with. In a way we want to live with our male partners, but not having each other in our lives would be hard. The ideal would be a situation where we live with each other and our male partners. From a boyfriend's perspective, you could look at our friendship as an in-law situation. But it hasn't been a source of tension. My boyfriend is thinking about buying a house; without me even prompting him, he assumed that both Jody and I would live there.

"Our life together really feels like a huge extended family, with people entering the picture and having the family grow. We have a lot of huge dinners at our house with anywhere from six to ten people. It does feel like a type of family around the table, but the roles are different from the nuclear family. There's not a typical mother, father, male, wife, husband. They're much more elusive roles, and they grow out of people's personalities."

When I shared Amy's story with my fellow QA analyst Reyhan, she asked me if I made it up. Their life sounds too perfect. It sounds like a quirkyalone utopia. Amy told me I could come to one of their dinners. I told her I would love to. A setup like theirs makes sense to me at an intuitive, gut level—far more than the sanctioned marital contract ever has.

Some people say that as you get older friendship inevitably becomes a less practiced art; with the crush of marriage, parenthood, career, and myriad responsibilities, friendship gets pushed to the end of the list. They lament the loss of those friendships. Maybe that is true for many people, but quirkyalones, whether we are parents or not, find it hard to imagine a life without friendship. For quirkyalones in their

"The older you get, the fewer slumber parties there are, and I hate that. I liked slumber parties. What happened to them?"
—Drew Barrymore, in an interview in *Cosmopolitan* magazine

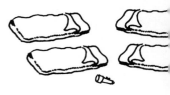

forties, fifties, sixties, and seventies, friendship can become even more important. The reality is that when we are sick and need help, a partner is not the only person who helps. Friendship can become even more important for single parents who lean on their friends for support.

No matter what our age, one permanent feature of a quirkyalone life is the desire for significant *others* in our lives. As we get older, the mainstream view asks us to shut down, to block these open passages to a variety of people, to make one partner and just a few people the center of our lives. It becomes weird in middle life (to a lesser extent in old age) to put friendship at the center of your life. The ultimate hope in a quirkyalone world is to make that less weird—to expand the range of connections and friendships that we can have at all stages of our lives.

Names: Christina Amini and Susan O'Malley

Ages: 26; 26

Hometowns: Ross, Calif.; San Jose, Calif.

Current Towns: San Anselmo, Calif.; San Francisco, Calif.

Favorite Golden Girl: Rose (both)

Personal QA motto: One of the defining characteristics of a quirkyalone is that you have significant others (quirkyalone friends) in your life. One quirkyalone + one quirkyalone + one quirkyalone + one quirkyalone = a quirkycluster. Quirkytogether is better.

Boston Marriages and Other Friendship Rites

In our time romantic love is the only song on the radio dial. We make romance a religion, the savior, the source of meaning in life, the only way to transcend the mundane or to be eternal. But many ancient thinkers—Aristotle and Cicero among them—considered romantic love random and viewed it as motivated by beauty, and they considered friendship a more powerful bond than blood relationships and romantic ties. According to historian John Boswell, the idea of being "just friends" would have been a paradox to Aristotle or Cicero; no relationship was more emotional, intimate, or intense.

Reverence for platonic friendship was not limited to ancient cultures. In nineteenth-century America, romantic friendships between women were often celebrated for their passionate qualities. Writing love letters, kissing, snuggling, and pledging eternal devotion were quite accepted among same-sex friends, as long as they didn't actually have sex. (See Pagan Kennedy's revival of Boston marriages, right.)

According to the Web site celebratefriendship.org, other cultures have had "formal customs regarding intense friendship. Native American cultures had 'blood brother' rituals. Hawaiian, Polynesian, and some African cultures even included a ritual of opposite-sex platonic friendship. (Thanks to this ritual, you could have both a spouse and an intense opposite-sex friend, each celebrated with a separate ceremony.) Some of these rituals granted friends the legal powers and responsibilities of blood family members."

What about friendship today? In her essay, "So . . . Are you Two Together?" published in *Ms.* in 2001, Pagan Kennedy, author of *Pagan Kennedy's Living: A Guide to Maturing Hipsters*, contemplated the complexities of friendship with her roommate, Liz. They both have boyfriends, but they have chosen to live together to share a home and build a life. They bought a decaying

Victorian together, they run several businesses and one non-profit group out of its rooms, go to parties as a couple, and spend holidays with each other's families. She re-flects that if they were lesbians, as people sometimes assume them to be, they would "fit more neatly into a box. But we're straight."

Because there is no appropriate language for their relationship (*roommate* doesn't cut it), Pagan Kennedy tells people that she and Liz are in a "Boston marriage," a phrase from the nineteenth century to describe a range of relationships in which women opted out of marriage and paired up to live together and maintain their freedom and independence. Sometimes Boston marriages were closeted lesbian relationships; often they were not. Kennedy describes the institution this way: "Most likely, the Boston marriage was many things to many women: business partnership, artistic collaboration, lesbian romance. And sometimes it was a friendship nurtured with all the care that we usually squander on our mates—a friendship as it could be if we made it the center of our lives."

WHAT TO DO WHEN A FRIEND STARTS SEEING SOMEONE: A FIVE-POINT PLAN

Watching a close friend embark on a new romantic relationship can involve a strange mix of emotions for a QA. In a tyranny-of-coupledom society, this should-be-happy occurrence taps into one of our greatest fears: that when a friend becomes coupled there no longer will be any room for us and that our treasured friendship will be sunk. Not to infantilize the quirkyalone, but the process can be similar to the experience of an only child getting a new sibling. At first, she or he fears being replaced. She or he even may be hostile to the new sibling (or boyfriend!). Eventually (usually), we learn there's enough love and attention to go around. Until then, the process can be difficult. That's where this book comes in. The following five-point plan will help you cope with the immediate feelings of loss, grief, or jealousy—and segue into a truly mature acceptance.

1. **Mourn the loss.** Don't try to pretend you have unconflicted emotions about your friend's sudden unavailability. You're not fooling anyone. Acknowledge that while the first reaction might be happiness, you also have sadness mixed with chagrin; you want to be excited for your friend, but you are worried about losing your partner in crime. It's okay. Sit with those feelings. Let them stew.

2. **Vent.** You need to express your fears of abandonment, but probably not to your friend. Talk with other members of your circle.

3. **Chill out.** Now that you have aired your anxieties, relax. In most cases the sexual frenzy will subside after the first few months and the friendship will resume. In the meantime, put

renewed emphasis on friends who are available and try not to lose perspective. You have not lost your friend—she is just mentally on vacation.

4. Assert yourself. If your friend truly disappears into the vortex, you have a decision to make: do you want to stage an intervention? Consider one or more of the following actions:

> Buy two tickets for a play, movie, or game. Announce that you want to see your friend independently—"just the two of us."
>
> Use positive reinforcement. Praise mutual friends who are in relationships but haven't fallen off the face of the Earth and are still as supportive, fun, and available as they always were.
>
> Open yourself to new possibilities. Friends are not replaceable or interchangeable. But if this individual is determined to spend all her or his time cocooning in bed, you may need to allow more kindred spirits into your life. Open yourself up to the possibilities of new friendships—especially with quirkyalones and quirkytogethers.

5. Let it run its course. Sometimes the only thing to do is nothing. Friendship, like romantic love, cannot be forced. You really can't stalk a friend. In most cases a friend will return from her seclusion. Or she may remain MIA. If the time is right, and the relationship is meant to continue, the friendship will evolve and return. When your friend comes back, she may be sheepish. She may be clueless. Brew a pot of tea, take a walk, or go out for a drink. And remember, ebbs and flows in a relationship are normal. They are part of the complicated yin-yang of long-term platonic commitment.

Name:
Scott Harrison Murray

Age: 25

Hometown: Boulder, Colo.

Current town: San Francisco,
Calif.

Job: Not-For-Profit Web
Worker

Length of time quirkyalone:
About four years

Name: Catherine Lunn

Age: 39

Hometown: New Orleans, La.

Current town: Kingston, N.Y.

Job: Director of Alumnae/i
Relations for Programs

Length of time quirkyalone:
thirty-nine years!

Favorite Golden Girl: Myself

Favorite quirkyalone activities:
Singing show tunes at the top
of my lungs and stargazing
on cold clear nights . . . not
simultaneously.

Name: Marty Zuckerman*

Age: 32

Hometown: New York, N.Y.

Current town: Cambridge,
Mass. (wah!)

Job: Scholar

Length of time quirkyslut:
Twelve years

Relationship status:
Eighteen-month relationship
(shattering previous record of
twelve months); girlfriend
recently introduced to parents;
cautiously optimistic

Favorite quirkyalone activity:
Photo booth pictures at
Lakeside Lounge, after 2 a.m.

*Pseudonym. The real Marty
feared that if he were to publicly
self-identify as a quirkyslut, he
might not have a promising
career in education.

Name: Mary Taylor

Age: 35

Hometown: Fair Oaks, Calif.

Current town: Sacramento, Calif.,
after stints in Santa Cruz and
Davis, Calif., the West Indies,
Austin, Tex., and Seattle, Wash.

Job: Librarian/Archivist; just
got laid off from my very cool
job because grant funding
ran out

Length of time quirkyalone:
Nine years; originally wanted
to "take time off" after ending
a frustrating relationship and
ended up learning how to
be comfortable with being
on my own

Favorite quirkyalone activities:
Traveling in Latin America,
yoga/pilates, swimming,
cooking, reading, napping

Personal QA motto: When I
was younger, I was very insecure
and would frequently end up in
all sorts of social relationships
(not just dating) where I'd be
with other people more out of
fear of loneliness than actually
enjoying their company. My
attitude now is that my social
relationships are driven by wanting to be with a specific person
(as friend or otherwise).

Quirkyalones in other eras
did not to try to destroy coupledom.
They simply wanted to be themselves.

Chapter eight
quirkyalones throughout history

HE world at large, especially the feminine world, is very prone to think that the unmarried woman remains so because no man has asked her

babies who believed so implicit Frances—why, that was impossible have been a woman if I could ha

I never married, because I neve whose love covered the faults in which I was sure would make r I never married, because since

PROFILES IN COURAGE

It should come as no surprise that we are experiencing the first massive emergence of quirkyalones now, as the daughters and sons of the second wave of feminism are coming into adulthood. As more women have entered the workforce, they have been able to gain economic independence, one of the key ingredients for quirkyalone liberation. When people have more of a choice about whether they want to be single or married, most romantic relationships are entered into at will, not by obligation. As sociologist Carol Gilligan told *Time,* in a cover story on the single woman's arrival, "There's now a pressure to create relationships that both men and women *want* to be in, and that's great! This is revolutionary."

Quirkyalones in other eras, by contrast, faced some tough battles. Consider the following quote from Paul Landis, a family advice expert from a decade as recent as the 1950s. "Except for the sick, the badly crippled, the deformed, the emotionally warped and the mentally defective, almost everyone has an opportunity (and by clear implication, a duty) to marry."

The amazing thing, however, is that even in the darkest of times, there have been individuals who have challenged prevailing social

Quirkyalone Thought to Ponder: According to *Reason* magazine, a 1965 survey found that more than 75 percent of college women said they would marry a man they didn't love "if he met their criteria for an ideal mate in every other respect." By 1991, about 90 percent of male and female college students said they would not marry someone they didn't love.

norms in the way they conducted their lives. The freedoms we take for granted today—the ability to keep our own last names when we marry, split household tasks among the genders, keep separate financial accounts, and go to the movies alone, among others—are in part the result of their struggles. The following profiles pay tribute to the quirkyalones of yore, individuals whose courage and vision have paved the way for us today.

Nina Simone—One of the most individual voices of the jazz era and, arguably, the least musically classifiable. In 1993 Don Shewey wrote of the "Priestess of Soul" in the *Village Voice*, "She's not a pop singer, she's a diva, a hopeless eccentric . . . who has so thoroughly co-mingled her odd talent and brooding temperament that she has turned herself into a force of nature, an exotic creature spied so infrequently that every appearance is legendary." Her songs, including "Backlash Blues," "Old Jim Crow," "Four Women," and "To Be Young, Gifted, and Black," were often adopted by the civil rights movement as anthems. The last was composed in honor of her friend Lorraine Hansberry; it became an anthem for the black power movement with its line "Say it clear, say it loud, I am black and I am proud!" Simone briefly married twice, once in 1958 and again in the late sixties, and had one daughter. Proving that love can come at any age for a quirkyalone, Simone had what she described as "a very intense love affair"—"it was like a volcano"—in her early sixties. Her last album was appropriately titled *A Single Woman,* and in it she meditated on the joys and sadness of her singular state. In the title track she sang of "A single woman out on a private cloud / Caught in a world few people understand."

Katharine Hepburn—Her autobiography was called *Me.* Her many movie roles indicate that she was drawn to playing independent women, misfits, and iconoclasts. She had a closeted, nearly three-decade affair with sometime costar Spencer Tracy. She said that although she fell for Tracy as if "hit over the head with a cast-iron skillet," she never wanted to marry him. Her final biographer, A. Scott Berg, who befriended the actress when she was seventy-five, suggests that there's truth to the notion that Hepburn was always attracted to men who were, if not married, at least somehow unmarriageable. "Living 'like a man,' as Kate often asserted—by herself, paying her own bills, and ultimately, answering to nobody—she liked that arrangement. . . ."

Brenda Ueland—Best known as the author of the inspirational book *If You Want to Write: A Book About Art, Independence, and Spirit*, originally published in 1938 and rereleased in 1987. The book encourages writers to trust their creative instincts and reassures with a democratic zeal that "everybody is talented, original, and has something to say," if they allow themselves to be honest on the page. Ueland spent her twenties in New York, where she was part of the Greenwich Village bohemian crowd that included John Reed, Louise Bryant, and others. After her first marriage ended and the Depression made the freelance lifestyle precarious, she returned with her daughter to Minneapolis, where she wrote and taught for over fifty years. *Strength to Your Sword Arm: Selected Writings* collects dozens of Ueland's newspaper columns, all ample evidence of the delight this writer took in her own iconoclasm. In "The Regrettable Herd Instinct" she wrote, "Sometimes people complain—my children and others—that I dress so unstylishly, so eccentrically, indeed so badly. I say this: 'If I did not wear torn pants, orthopedic shoes, frantic disheveled hair, that is to say, if I did not tone down my beauty, people would go mad. Married men would run amuck.'" Ueland married and divorced three times. Like another female quirkyalone of the twentieth century, Ueland also titled her 1947 autobiography *Me*. Some have speculated that she might have liked to tease Katharine Hepburn about this imitation. (Ueland used the title first.)

Sei Shonagan—A court lady in tenth-century Japan, Sei Shonagan was the author of *The Pillow Book*, a list maker's dream of a book, in which she cataloged memories of court and religious ceremonies, character sketches, places that interested her, diary entries, lists of things she loathed and enjoyed, descriptions of nature, pilgrimages, poetry exchanges—almost everything that made up daily life for the upper classes in Japan during the Heian period. (Her rival Lady Murasaki, whose novel *The Tale of Genji* fictionalizes the court life Shonagan describes, was also something of a quirkyalone. A well-respected writer summoned to the imperial court for her talents, she kept out of the limelight, preferring solitude, but remained keenly observant.)

Shonagan was a maverick, unapologetically outspoken and opinionated. In her work—what we might now call creative nonfiction—she exhibits the perfectionism of the quirkyalone in howlingly funny detail. In fact, in "Hateful Things," she writes a precursor to one of the lists that appears in this book, "Deal Breakers." Her style is so eloquent, her observations so skillfully chosen, and her wit so sharp that even the smallest details jump off the page. Following is just a small sample of "Hateful Things":

- A man who has nothing in particular to recommend him discusses all sorts of subjects at random as though he knew everything.

- One has been foolish enough to invite a man to spend the night in an unsuitable place—and then he starts snoring.

- One is telling a story about old times when someone breaks in with a little detail that he happens to know, implying that one's own version is inaccurate—disgusting behavior!

- Very hateful is a mouse that scurries all over the place.

- A lover who is leaving at dawn announces that he has to find his fan and his paper. "I know I put them somewhere last night," he says. Since it is pitch dark, he gropes about the room, bumping into the furniture and muttering, "Strange! Where on earth can they be?" Finally he discovers the objects. He thrusts the paper into the breast of his robe with a great rustling sound; then he snaps open the fan and busily fans away with it. Only now is he ready to take his leave. What charmless behavior! "Hateful" is an understatement!

"I think Groundhog Day is a QA movie, at least until the happy-couple ending. Basically, the main character learns that he is alone in the world and that he must learn to find interests and activities that are satisfying to him alone. He goes ➛

James Baldwin—A consummate outsider, Baldwin experimented with love, always advocated universal brotherhood, and created his own possibilities. Despite the prominent role he played in the civil rights movement, not only writing about race relations but also organizing protest actions, Baldwin always rejected the labels of leader or spokesman. In an interview published in the *New York Times* he said, "I was a maverick, a maverick in the sense that I depended on neither the white world nor the black world. . . . The fact that I went to Europe so early is probably what saved me. It gave me another touchstone—myself." In addition to writing about race, Baldwin dealt with other taboo themes, among them homosexuality and interracial relationships. His groundbreaking 1956 novel, *Giovanni's Room,* depicted a young man in Paris grappling with his sexual identity. It's intensely passionate, recommended reading for any quirkyalone. During his long career, Baldwin never concealed his sexuality. He rejected the label gay, saying that he was open to love regardless of what form or gender it might take.

Abigail Adams—Wife of one president, mother to another, and half of the first quirkytogether couple in the White House. Much of what we know about her intense, playful relationship with John Adams comes from the more than 1,100 letters they exchanged, beginning during their courtship in 1762 and continuing throughout John's political career. In an era when daily life and survival could be all-consuming, she was not only a mother to five, but also a

MOVIES TO WATCH

Suggestions for a quirkyalone movie night.

Amelie
Amy's O (not so great, but extremely QA, almost scarily so)
Annie Hall
A Single Girl
Batman (or *Spider-Man*)*
Blade Runner
Crouching Tiger, Hidden Dragon
Crush
Ghost World
Hideous Kinky
Holiday
How Stella Got Her Groove Back
Kissing Jessica Stein
Little Women
Never Been Kissed
Next Stop Wonderland
Punch-Drunk Love
Raising Victor Vargas
Romy and Michele's High School Reunion
Rushmore
Titanic (Yes! Quirkyalones refuse to deny the power of the epic, the value in being swept away.)
Walking and Talking
Yentl

*Andrew Boyd explains, "Almost all the male-vigilante-crime-crusader-type figures are quirkyalone."

"I nominate all cheesy teen movies. Because at the same time as they vigorously reinforce superficial values, they tend to always have some token lesson about how you just need to be yourself, and I am a sap so I ingest that lesson and ignore the rest."—Rowan Millar, San José, Calif.

through three distinct stages: live for the moment, then nihilism, then acceptance of the fact that we all must live and die fundamentally alone. Maybe quirkyalones go through these stages as well."—Ethan Watters, San Francisco, Calif.

competent farm manager and financial overseer. She witnessed the American Revolution up close and extrapolated its meaning for women in her letters. On March 31, 1776, she wrote to her husband, "I long to hear that you have declared an independency. And, by the way, in the new code of laws, which I suppose it will be necessary for you to make, I desire you would remember the ladies and be more generous and favorable to them than your ancestors. . . . Remember, all men would be tyrants if they could. If particular care and attention is not paid to the ladies, we are determined to foment a rebellion, and will not hold ourselves bound by any laws in which we have no voice or representation."

Jesus—What about Jesus? Was the divine son of a virgin mother a quirkyalone? In some ways, Jesus' life did not fit the mold: his life was almost preprogrammed; he was living for everyone but himself. But in other ways, when you start to examine the details of his life, it's hard to think of anything but QA. Although Jesus embodied agape, a broad love of humanity, he chose his friends carefully and he liked to retreat from society with them. He also needed to spend time alone. After Jesus fed five thousand people with five loaves and two fishes, the people wanted to make him a king. Instead, Jesus took off alone to a mountaintop. Jesus didn't want accolades; he wanted time to reflect. Jesus had a consuming, unconventional mission in life. He was tempted by the devil to be the king of all empires, but he rejected these offers in favor of becoming a radical populist—he lived and died on his own independent path, building a new proselytizing world religion that became Christianity. What would Jesus do? Would Jesus have self-identified as a quirkyalone? It's hard to say. But there is a certain comfort in considering that the son of God might have been one of us.

PROFILE IN COWARDLINESS

Rainer Maria Rilke—Considered by many to be one of the greatest lyric poets of twentieth-century German literature, and definitely a poet for modern times, Rilke is often cited in personal ads and in movies (see *Kissing Jessica Stein*) as a code word for romantic individualists. In his poetry Rilke expresses the truth that going deeply into ourselves can make us, paradoxically, better prepared to love other human beings. For many quirkyalones, *Letters to a Young Poet* is the original self-help book. (Written between 1903 and 1908, *Letters* is the result of a correspondence between Rilke and a young would-be poet and soldier, who wrote to Rilke for advice about his writing after being "touched by a sympathetic note in one of his poems.")

At the risk of seeming like a jilted, deceived lover, I must share the truth about this man. A May 8, 2000, *New Republic* article by Brian Phillips, "The Angel and the Egotist: The Human Cost of Rilke's Art," exposed the cult that has developed around the poet in part because of the mystical authority that many readers find in his poems. The article reveals that his behavior was far less inspirational than his writing.

Six months after his daughter was born, Rilke abandoned his wife, Clara, and moved to Paris. He invited Clara to participate in an "interior" marriage that would not require him to be physically present as a husband or a father. He used

funds set aside for his daughter's education for his own housing needs, and he continued throughout adulthood in a pattern of dishonest love-them-and-leave-them behavior. He started love affairs with many artistic and intellectual women. When he left them, he always said that he didn't want to hurt them but that his poetry required total freedom.

The translator's note to *Letters* hints that Rilke may not have lived up to the ideals he preached: "It is evident that a great artist, whatever the immediate conditions disturbing his own life, may be able to clarify for the benefit of another those fundamental truths. . . . Though Rilke expresses himself with a wisdom and a kindness that seem to reflect the calm of self-possession, his spirit may have been speaking out of its own need rather than from the security of ends achieved, so that his words indeed reflect desire rather than fulfillment."

For Rilke, solitude and freedom were vital; they fueled his work and his spirit. But he also used solitude as an excuse for bad behavior. In his writing he was a quirkyalone. In his life he may have been a quirkyasshole.

FIRST AWAKENINGS OF THE QUIRKYALONE MOVEMENT

It's hard to believe that the quirkyalone movement was getting started over a hundred years ago. As early as 1885, *Ladies' Home Journal* published articles signed by authors with names such as "A Spinster Who Has Learned to Say No," and "A Happy Old Maid." What's amazing is how contemporary the voices in these articles sound (three are excerpted for your reading pleasure, on page 129).

How on earth did these articles make it to the light of day, reaching thousands of American readers? *Ladies' Home Journal and Practical Housekeeper* was not a radical feminist magazine or a small press. It launched in 1883; by 1886 its circulation had reached four hundred thousand, and it was the most widely read women's magazine of the nineteenth century. The fact that *Ladies' Home Journal* published confessional essays from women who would not content themselves with "an inferior article of husband merely for the sake of being married" reflected changing mores of the day. In previous eras of American history, and during most of the twentieth century, the condition of being a spinster or old maid was viewed as at best pitiable and at worst sinful. But during the years 1880 to 1920, the industrial revolution and urbanization were well under way; doors to higher education opened to women, and so did many career opportunities. Changing social conditions made the spinster a temporary icon of female self-sufficiency and independence, with even a touch of glamour, not unlike QAs today.

For more on these amazing historical artifacts, see Naomi Braun Rosenthal's *Spinster Tales and Other Womanly Possibilities* (State University of New York Press, 2002).

WHY I NEVER MARRIED.

By An Old Maid.

THE world at large, especially the feminine world, is very prone to think that the unmarried woman remains so because no man has asked her to become his wife. This is not so. Any woman who is pleasant to look upon, cheerful in her manners, and neat in her mode of dressing, has

...y opportunities to marry ; we all know of ...less, unattractive, untidy women who also ...ry ; therefore, when somebody says to me ...ho am forty, healthy, said to be good-look-...well-educated and always well-dressed—...wonder why you never married ?" or, mur-...r, "Curious that nobody ever wanted Miss ...—," I simply smile and wonder that ...men can't see better into the hearts of other ...en.

...y friends, every woman in this world ...wants to marry. It is true, she may

the man I loved unt... would have worked ... I would have adapte... and associations of t... strong, but that I s... people, that I shou... babies who believed... Frances—why, that w... have been a woman i...

I never married, b... whose love covered w... which I was sure w... I never married, be... twenty-five years old... much that it seemed... not believe that mar... my existence. I did ... have left lonely two... would have heard n... but for me ; they w... duced to go out in the... there to persuade, an... no hand was as soo... when illness came, t... quite so good as th... for them, and tha... much for them as ... sisters had husban... quently father and ... first. But every Su... that one command ... and mother, and thy...

this one could have been printed today ←

From February 1891,
Ladies' Home Journal

Woman in the Year 2000
By Edward Bellamy

From November 1890,
Ladies' Home Journal

Why I Never Married
By an Old Maid

WOMAN IN THE YEAR
2000

By Edward Bellamy

(*Author of "Looking Backward," etc., etc.*)

...T is assumed that the year 2000 will see Nationalism fully established as the basis of the industrial system and of society, so far as depend ent upon it. Judging from the signs of the times I think it would be quite safe to make the date seventy-five years earlier, but for the benefit of those weak in the faith it is set well ahead. As there are doubtless some who do not understand very clearly what Nationalism is, it may be well enough just here to explain, so far as may be done in a phrase, that it proposes turning over all the business of the country to a single firm, of which all the people, women as well as men, shall be employés, and in the proceeds of which all shall be equal partners. Leaving wholly aside, for the present purpose, all explanations as to the details of this plan, and all questions as to its feasibility, it is simply proposed to point out certain ways in which the position of women would be affected by its successful introduction.

We are to suppose that every adult woman in the United States—while required, like every adult man (except as modified by sex conditions), to perform some self-elected useful work—had coming to her a regular annual income in the form of credit, to be expended as she pleased, equal, say, to the present purchasing power of $1000, $3000 or $5000, more or less, according to the prosperity of the national firm, said income to be the same in amount with that received by her brother, husband or father, but not to come to her through them or through any other intermediary, but directly ...ministration, as a matter

...that woman, ...disqualifi-...en, as a ...on the ...of a ...ent to ...

...sumption referred to by making marri...to another.

Would you gain a realization of the position of the "old maid" in the year 2000? If so, ...o more obviously desirable to one sex tha... look at the lordly bachelor of to-day, the hero of romance, the cynosure of the drawing-room and of the promenade. Even as that bright being, like him self-poised, serenely *insouciant*, free as air, will the "old maid" of the year 2000 be. It is altogether probable, by the way, that the term "old maid" will by that time have fallen into disuse.

But while the unmarried woman of the year 2000, whether young or old, will enjoy the dignity and independence of the bachelor of to-day, the insolent prosperity at present en- joyed by the latter will have passed into ...lutary, if sad, eclipse. No longer profiti... the effect of the pressure of economic ...onalism ...t upon woman, to make him indis...nd. That ...dependent exclusively up...er rights as a ...tions, instead of ...national concern. ...pen...heir husbands, of being obliged to ask for all they have, beyond bare bread and meat, which the best and noblest of wives now have to endure, the wife of the year 2000 would never know.

Let us suppose, on the other hand, that her heart, remaining untouched, she had preferred to remain single.

At the present time, a popular presumption exists that all girls wish to marry, and fail to do so only because they lack an eligible opportunity. This presumption exists on account of the obvious fact that women, being able with difficulty to support themselves, have in general a greater material interest in marriage then men have. Surely there can be few in-cidents of an unmarried woman's condition more exasperating than her knowledge that because this is the undeniable fact it is in vain for her to expect to be popularly credited with the voluntary choice of celibacy. The maid must endure with a smile, however she may rage within, the coarse jest or innuendo to which she would be none than vain to reply. Nationalism, by establishing the economic in-dependence of women, without reference to their single or married state, will destroy the

---

...m July 1885, *Ladies' Home Journal*

...y They Do Not Marry
...Young Woman Explains a
...ial Problem.

...a small party of workers and thinkers a ... nights ago, I was in a group that dis-...sed the distaste for marriage which ...racterizes the girlhood of the day. One ...ng lady has fortified herself with a ...wspaper clipping on the subject, which ... drew from her pocket and read, as fur-...r substantiating her position. It was to ... effect that husband-hunting maidens, ...ng or old, were much scarcer than of ...e ; that instead of being anxious to marry, ...s were slow of inducement to that direc-...

It is true," said the young lady. "I scarce-...know a girl who wants to marry. They ... learning something in the way of a pro-...sion, something that will interest them as ...l as support them, two roles in which ...bands just now fail. The truth is, we are ...scared away from any desire to marry by ...ing how wretched those who do marry ... Where would we look for husbands? ...ong the 'snips' and 'sports' and charac-...ess young men that fill our drawing-...ms! They are insufferable as mere

acquaintances or beaus; who could con-template them as husbands? I have always thought that if I could find a young man at all like my father I could love and marry him; but that school of men has van-ished from the younger ranks."

Nobody doubts that she expressed the convictions of a large representation of young women. Their lack of interest in marriage is not due to the larger activities which continually open before women, but the unat-tractive, unreliable material in the way of husbands. Women are women, and would love and marry as readily today as when the earth was new, if they came in contact with men who aroused their respect and admiration. The order of maidenhood that could content itself with an inferior article of husband, merely for the sake of being married, has almost vanished. The young woman of the period has too much character and self-respect to dread being an old maid so much that she would contract an uncongenial union to escape it.

quirkyalone: *yes or no?*

Aimee Mann: Yes. *Til Tuesday*'s "Voices Carry" reminds us never to be silent in a relationship.

Alanis Morissette: Yes. With "You Oughta Know," Alanis makes it clear that hell hath no fury like a quirkyalone scorned.

Ally McBeal: Controversial but yes. The poster child for long walks alone at night.

Alyssa Milano: No.

Angelina Jolie: Yes, but only recently.

Anne Hutchinson: Yes. A religious rebel who challenged the very basis for the Puritan colony by preaching that God's grace was implanted in every human soul.

> "Figure out who you are separate from your family and the man or woman you're in a relationship with. . . . I think that's the most important thing in life. Find a sense of self because with that, you can do anything else."—as told to *Cosmopolitan*

Ashton Kutcher: *no !* He gets the award for most offensively unquirkyalone celebrity. Exploits fake relationships to get publicity in a most obvious way.

Ben Affleck: No.

Bjork: Yes. Often sings about maintaining your own space while you're in a relationship.

Bridget Jones: *nope.* Too concerned about calories. Relationships should be fostered, not festered.

Britney Spears: *hmmm* . . . Tough call. There's something scarily manufactured and artificial about her (it would be hard to call her quirky), but in these post–Justin Timberlake days she does seem to be embracing being untethered and open to possibility. In a probing *US Weekly* article, "Why Isn't Britney Dating?" she says, "It's more exciting when you don't have a boyfriend."

Cher: Yes. (Post-Sonny.)

Cleopatra: Yes. Ruled Egypt in her own rather than the name of her husband.

Courtney Cox: No. Uses relationship with David Arquette to shill Coca-Cola.

Courtney Love: No.

David Sedaris: Probably would not want a label, but yes.

Elizabeth Cady Stanton: Yes. Quirkytogether and also very friend-focused. She collaborated with Susan B. Anthony to advocate for women's suffrage.

Erykah Badu: Yes.

Frances McDormand: Yes, plays complex, non-traditional female leads.

Freddie Prinze Jr.: No.

Frederick Douglass: *yes* Uncompromising abolitionist.

Meg Ryan and Tom Hanks:
The enemies of quirkyalones everywhere

Gisele: No.

Jamie Lee Curtis: Yes. Purposely showed off her flabby areas in a photo shoot to show herself as a "real" person.

Janeane Garofalo: *yes!*

Janet Reno: Yes.

Joan of Arc: Yes. Followed her inner voice in the face of scorn and ridicule.

Kate Winslet: Yes. Consistently plays female characters on journeys of self-exploration.

Katharine Hepburn: Yes. Introduced an entirely new type of female character.

Keri Russell: Only as Felicity (now-canceled cult favorite show about a girl who followed her crush to New York for college).

Kramer: Yes.

Laverne and Shirley: Yes. Real and unafraid to show it. Plus, friendship is very important to quirkyalones.

Margaret Cho:

yes!

She's the one that she wants.

Mary Magdalene: Yes. Who wouldn't hold out for the Messiah?

Mary Wollstonecraft: Yes.

Meg Ryan and Tom Hanks: *no!, no!, no!* The enemies of quirkyalones everywhere.

Muhammad: No. *(Conqueror or together)*

Morrissey: Yes. For those who grew up in the eighties, the prototypical quirkyalone.

Nicole Kidman: *maybe.* Often goes to her movie premieres alone, sometimes brings her sister and friends.

Oprah: *of course.*

Oscar Wilde: Yes.

Pat Sajak: Probably not.

Phoebe: Yes.

Queen Latifah: *yes*

Ralph Nader: Yes. Obeys his inner voice, even under extreme pressure.

Saicho: Yes. A monk at the age of thirteen, Saicho (767–822) was among the first to make being quirkyalone a required and valued discipline. In order to excel at Saicho's school of Buddhism, monks had to spend at least twelve years in isolation, gaining better knowledge of the self.

Salma Hayek: Yes.

Sandra Bernhard: Yes. Quirkyalone *and* bisexual. *(Extra points!)*

Sarah Jessica Parker: Yes. Has made a career out of playing the misfits and oddballs, starting with the brainy, awkward Patty Greene on *Square Pegs.*

Shannon Doherty: No.

Soleil Moon Frye: Yes (as Punky Brewster).

Steve Martin: Yes.

Thora Birth: Yes (for Enid in *Ghost World*).

Tina Turner: Yes. Archetypal late-blooming quirkyalone who has been there, done that, and recreated her life from scratch.

Walt Whitman: Yes.

Wonder Woman: Yes.

Woody Allen: No. Quirkycreepy.

"I know I'm supposed to differentiate between the character and the person, but anyone who's seen <u>Pump up the Volume</u> knows that Christian Slater is a lovely quirkyalone."— Holly, quirkyalone

RESOURCES
Because no quirkyalone is an island.

Alternatives to Marriage Project (www.unmarried.org)
Information, advocacy, and support for people who are living together before marriage, choose not to marry, cannot marry, or are questioning marriage and seeking information as they make their decision.

American Association of Single People (www.singlesrights.com)
Should the White House push welfare recipients to marry? The American Association of Single People says no. Education and advocacy for America's 86 million unmarried and single adults, including solo singles, single parents, domestic partners, roommates, and unmarried families.

Bitchmagazine.com
Pop culture analysis from a quirkyalone-friendly perspective.

Celebratefriendship.org
A clearinghouse of information about friendship: advice, history, and anthropology.

Coabode.com
A matchmaking service that provides single mothers the opportunity to share housing while pooling resources and finances with another single mom of their choosing. (Hello *Kate and Allie!*)

Hipmama.com
A magazine and Web site for breeders, filled with political commentary and tales from the front lines of motherhood. Started as a forum for young mothers, single parents, and marginalized voices, it has grown to represent progressive families of all kinds.

Indiebride.com
Alternative views on marriage process: the highs, the lows, and the complexities.

Insanityhouse.com
A nonprofit that aims to unite single-parent families in the United States and, through a unified voice, challenge current legislation and change political policy.

International Couples' Resources
(members.fortunecity.com/canzian/Resources.html)
Resources for people who are married or engaged to someone of a different nationality.

Human Rights Campaign Fund Worknet
(www.hrc.org/worknet/dp/index.asp)
A list of employers that provide domestic partner benefits.

(continued on page 134)

STATE OF INDIANA

EXECUTIVE DEPARTMENT
INDIANAPOLIS

PROCLAMATION

Executive Order

To All To Whom These Presents May Come, Greeting:

WHEREAS, the recent U. S. census found that 86 million adults in the United States are not married; that 47 percent of the nation's households are headed by unmarried adults; and that a majority of households in 13 states and 300 cities are headed by unmarried adults; and

WHEREAS, the living arrangements of unmarried Americans are diverse, with 27 million adults living alone, nearly 10 million single parents living with and raising children and 45 million adults living with unmarried adult family members or in other types of unmarried households; and

WHEREAS, unmarried men and women make significant contributions to society in a wide variety of ways – as productive employees, as loving family members, as good neighbors and as dedicated volunteers in civic and charitable causes; and

WHEREAS, Unmarried America, the membership division of the American Association for Single People, is a leading provider of information and resources for and about unmarried Americans and, through its educational programs, the association works to improve the quality of life and secure a better future for this population; and

WHEREAS, Unmarried America is commemorating the third week of September as Unmarried and Single Americans Week (USA Week);

NOW, THEREFORE, I, FRANK O'BANNON, Governor of the State of Indiana, do hereby proclaim September 21-27, 2003,

UNMARRIED AND SINGLE AMERICANS WEEK

in the State of Indiana, and invite all citizens to take due note of the observance.

IN TESTIMONY WHEREOF, I have hereunto set my hand and caused to be affixed the Great Seal of the State of Indiana at the Capitol in Indianapolis on this 20th. day of August, 2003.

Frank O'Bannon

BY THE GOVERNOR: Frank O'Bannon
Governor of Indiana

Todd Rokita

ATTEST: Todd Rokita
Secretary of State

The American Association of Single People has declared its own holiday to push for rights and respect for unmarried Americans. National USA (Unmarried and Single American) Week is the third week of September. Fringe holiday? Governors of California, Indiana, Minnesota, Maine, Nevada, Rhode Island, and more have issued proclamations of support.

Leatherspinsters.com
A Web site for happily unmarried straight or asexual women.

Lucystoneleague.org
Dedicated to name-choice freedom (equal rights for women and men to retain, modify, and create their names, because a person's name is fundamental to her or his existence).

Meetup.com
A free service to help you organize local gatherings about anything, anywhere. Perhaps a tool for QAs to get together.

Singlefathers.org
A resource for all types of single fathers—noncustodial, custodial, or widowed.

Singlemothers.org
Support and information for women who are considering, or who have chosen, single motherhood.

To-Do List (www.todolistmagazine.com)
The original voice of the quirkyalone. Information will be posted on this Web site as well as quirkyalone.com regarding future celebrations of International Quirkyalone Day. Also, looking for investors! If interested, contact the publisher (me).

Universal Health Care Action Network
(www.uhcan.org)
Advocates for comprehensive, affordable, and publicly accountable health care for all in the U.S., regardless of employment or relationship status.

Ten quirkyalone songs to sing at karaoke

Sinead O'Connor, "I Do Not Want What I Haven't Got"

REM, "Walk Unafraid"

Standard, "All or Nothing at All"

The Supremes, "You Can't Hurry Love"

Frank Sinatra, "My Way"

Nina Simone, "A Single Woman"

Erykah Badu, "My Apple Tree"

Jill Scott, "One Is the Magic Number"

Liz Phair, "Polyester Bride"

Whitesnake, "Here I Go Again"

QUIRKYALONE READING LIST

Suggestions for further reading from my bookshelf and QAs nationwide.

A Room of One's Own by Virginia Woolf
All About Love: New Visions by bell hooks
The Book of Phoebe by Mary-Ann Tirone Smith
Can Love Last?: The Fate of Romance over Time
   by Stephen Mitchell
The Company She Keeps by Mary McCarthy
Eccentrics: A Study of Sanity and Strangeness
   by David Weeks
The Exes by Pagan Kennedy (read it for Walt, an
   extremely QA indie rocker)
The Four Loves by C. S. Lewis (for insights on
   friendship)
The Girl with the Silver Eyes by Willo Davis Roberts
The House of Mirth by Edith Wharton (Lily Bart:
   tragic quirkyalone)
The Perks of Being a Wallflower by Stephen
   Chbosky
The Long Goodbye by Raymond Chandler (and all
   of his Phillip Marlowe detective novels)
*The Lost Soul Companion: A Book of Comfort and
   Constructive Advice for Black Sheep, Square
   Pegs, Struggling Artists, and Other Free Spirits*
   by Susan M. Brackney
The Missing Piece Meets the Big O by Shel
   Silverstein
I, The Divine: A Novel in First Chapters by
   Rabih Alameddine
Journal of a Solitude by May Sarton
*Love Undetectable: Notes on Friendship, Sex, and
   Survival* by Andrew Sullivan
Object of My Affection by Stephen McCauley
   (The movie version is not nearly as good.)
Revolutionary Road by Richard Yates (as cautionary
   tale)
Self-Help by Lorrie Moore (indeed, almost all of
   Lorrie Moore)
"*Self Reliance*" by Emerson
Strength to Your Sword Arm: Collected Writings
   by Brenda Ueland
*The Way We Never Were: American Families
   and the Nostalgia Trap* by Stephanie Coontz

The Temple of My Familiar
by Alice Waters

"Essential reading for QAs. A magic book whose narrative takes place over thousands of years and many continents. Couples break up only to become more alive, complete, and able to be their fullest, authentic, sparkling selves. They are able to love, form new relationships, and reconnect with old loves in a healing way." —William Poy Lee, Berkeley, Calif.

The Vagabond by Colette

Beth Stein of Seattle writes, "If you haven't read *The Vagabond*, you must. Colette has some great lines about relationships and solitude."

The White Album and *Slouching Towards Bethlehem*

"All Joan Didion seems QA to me; that sense of having a little distance from the goings-on around you. Like Didion, the QA is often the best observer of the machinations of society." —Ethan Watters, San Francisco, Calif.

Name: Linda McEvoy

Age: 30

Hometown: Dublin, Ire.

Current Town: Dublin, Ire.

Job: Lawyer and actor

Length of time quirkyalone:
twenty-nine years (quirkyslut:
one and a half years)

Favorite quirkyalone activities:
Eating in top restaurants,
going to cinema, traveling on
the Bateau Mouche in Paris, a
romantic solo night in listening
to Erykah Badu and Jazzanova

MANY VOICES, ONE COMMUNITY

Name: Rosemary Pepper

Age: 35

Hometown: Philadelphia, Pa.

Current town: San Francisco, Calif.

Job: Writer

Length of time in support of
quirkyalones: Forever

Relationship status: We've been
together for thirteen years (in a
row!) and married for three.

Favorite quirkyalone activities:
Curling up with the dog and
a DVD, home spa treatments,
mani/pedis, glitter, crafts,
magazines, dining alone in
utter decadence.

Personal QA motto: Aside from
dumb luck and great timing, I
attribute much of the success of
our relationship to the fact that
we are extremely independent as
individuals. We're not looking to
fill some weird hole or to com-
pensate for what each of us may
lack. We simply realize that being
together makes each of us better.
What makes us fun at parties is
that we work the room on our
own terms, and not as an arm-
locked wall of couple or as
people making out in the corner
all night.

quirkyalones throughout history · quirkyalones throughout hist

136

Name: Michelle Thomas

Age: 27

Hometown: Houston, Tex.

Current town: Houston, Tex.

Job: Land Tech, Land Admin.
Dept.

Length of time quirkyalone:
Two years

Favorite Golden Girl: Dorothy

Favorite quirkyalone activities:
Movies, gallery openings,
book signings

Personal QA motto: Stolen from
Some Kind of Wonderful: "I'd
rather be alone for the right
[reasons], than with someone for
the wrong."*

*Several people have sent this quote
from *Some Kind of Wonderful* as
their motto. Interestingly, a viewing
of the film reveals that the line is
actually the opposite: "I'd rather be
with someone for the wrong reasons
than be alone for the right."

Name: Lynda

Age: 34

Hometown: Baltimore, Md.

Current town: Baltimore, Md.

Job: Technical Writer

Length of time quirkyalone:
All my life

Relationship status: Currently
having illicit affair with myself

Favorite Golden Girl: Sophia

Favorite quirkyalone activities:
Knitting, crocheting, watching
movies, walking my dog

Personal QA motto: Never
compare your inside to somebody else's outside. And never
settle for somebody whose
company you enjoy less than
your dog's.

PORTRAIT OF THE ARTIST AS A YOUNG QUIRKYALONE

The author wrote and illustrated the following tale at the age of thirteen. When she rediscovered it in a long-packed-away cardboard box at age twenty-six, she found eerie similarities to the writing she did in her twenties—and to the subject of this book.

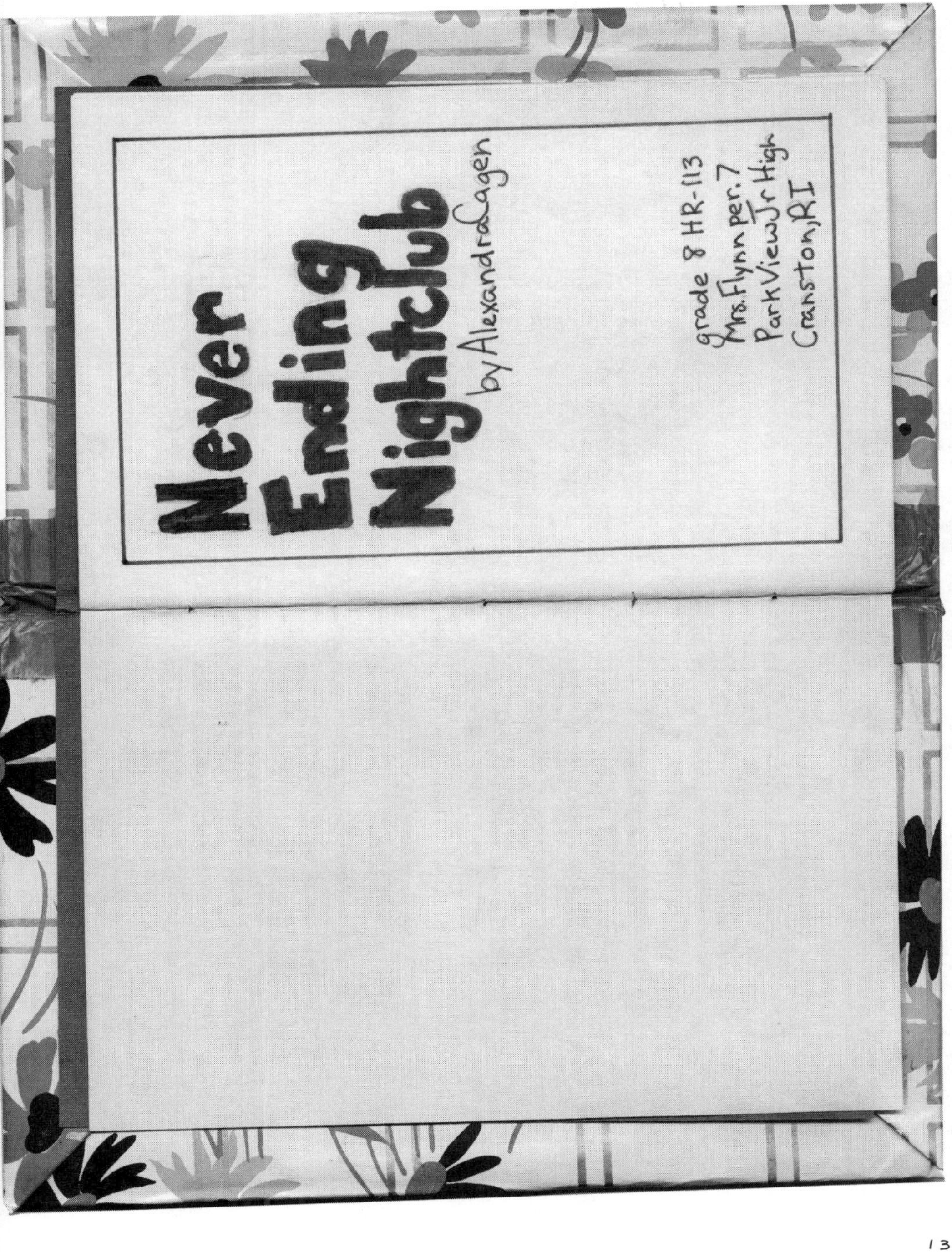

Never Ending Nightclub

by Alexandra Cagen

grade 8 HR-113
Mrs. Flynn per. 7
ParkView Jr High
Cranston, RI

139

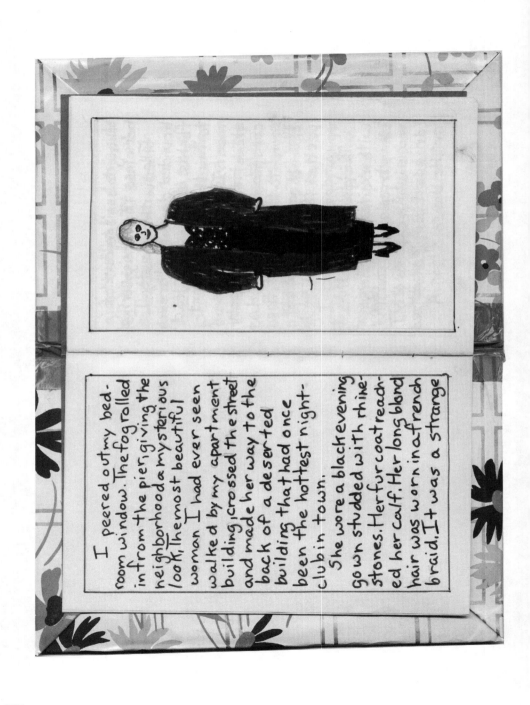

I peered out my bedroom window. The fog rolled in from the pier, giving the neighborhood a mysterious look. The most beautiful woman I had ever seen walked by my apartment building, crossed the street and made her way to the back of a deserted building that had once been the hottest nightclub in town.

She wore a black evening gown studded with rhinestones. Her fur coat reached her calf. Her long blond hair was worn in a french braid. It was a strange thing to see someone of her class in my neighborhood. Filled with curiosity, I bounded down the three flights of stairs that lead to my three-room apartment. I ran across the street trying not to look conspicuous. I walked around to the back of the crumbling building and peeked into a half-boarded up window.

The place was alive with excitement. A huge orchestra played beautiful music while expensively dressed couples waltzed on the dance floor. A giant buffet lined one side of the room. It served delicacies such as caviar and champagne.

I was intrigued. Why were they in this deserted building? I had never seen these people before. Why weren't their Cadillacs and Mercedes on the street? This was so strange! I was perplexed.

I ran as quickly as my feet would take me back home. I called my best friend Annie as soon as I reached my telephone.

"Hello!", Annie said.

"Annie, come over here

right now! I have to show you something really weird!"

"What are you talking about? Speak slower."

"Listen, just meet me in front of my house in fifteen minutes."

"Alright. Bye."

Fifteen minutes later we were standing on my sidewalk.

"Come on," I told her as I led her to the half-boarded window. We looked in and found that the place which was a high class night club just fifteen minutes ago

was now just a huge mess of dust, old tables and a broken-down bar.

"This isn't right! I was just here! It was a great night club. There was an orchestra! People were dancing!"

"What is wrong with you? It's just the same old deserted place it always was. Is this a joke?"

"No, Annie! I swear, I'm telling the truth. I was just here twenty minutes ago."

"You didn't bump your head, did you?"

"Annie, don't humor me!"

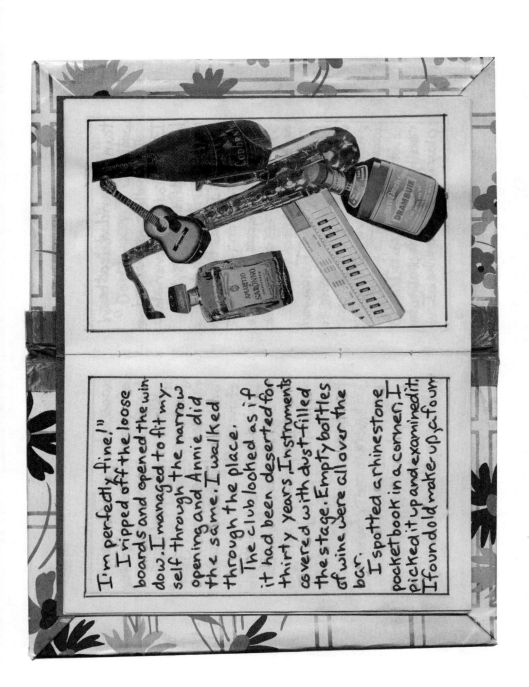

I'm perfectly fine!"
I ripped off the loose boards and opened the window. I managed to fit myself through the narrow opening, and Annie did the same. I walked through the place.

The club looked as if it had been deserted for thirty years. Instruments covered with dust filled the stage. Empty bottles of wine were all over the bar.

I spotted a rhinestone pocketbook in a corner. I picked it up and examined it. I found old makeup, a fountain pen and a leather wallet.

The wallet interested me. It contained seven dollars and fifty cents, two credit cards and a driver's license. It was the woman's license. It gave her name, street address and phone number.

"Annie, look!" I showed her the license. "Come on, I want to get to a phone. I have to call this woman."

"Alright, alright, I'm not really too thrilled about playing detective. I

have a date tonight."

"Don't worry. I won't mess up your precious hair."

We returned to my apartment with the pocketbook. I dialed the phone number.

"Hello," answered an old-ish sounding woman.

"Hello. Does a woman by the name of Bridgette Shivenson live here? I have something that belongs to her."

"Bridgette is my daughter. She died over five years ago. What do you have of hers?"

"She's dead?! I just saw her an hour ago. I have her pocketbook."

"Listen, I don't appreciate these crank calls! Her death caused me a lot of pain. Don't you understand that? Now good bye!"

I just sat there stunned for a few minutes. What is happening with me?

"Look, I don't know what's wrong with you," said Annie. "Maybe you should go home and rest. I've got to go. My date's picking me up at seven. Call me tomorrow."

"Yeah, okay, I'll talk to you then."

I sat down and thought about the day's extremely bizarre events. I decided to see if I had been dreaming my visions of the nightclub. I squeezed into the prom dress I wore five years ago, slipped into high heels and fixed my hair and make-up.

I walked over to the building and went around to the back. Peering through the window, I could see the same orchestra and place as

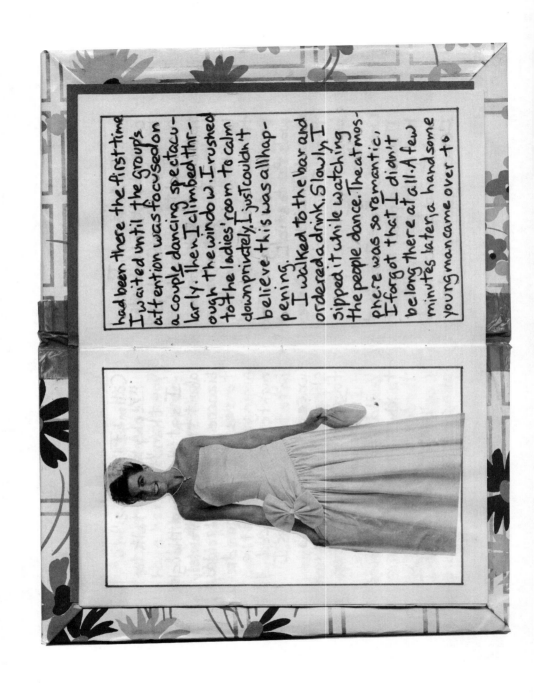

had been there the first time. I waited until the group's attention was focused on a couple dancing spectacularly. Then I climbed through the window. I rushed to the ladies' room to calm down privately. I just couldn't believe this was all happening.

I walked to the bar and ordered a drink. Slowly, I sipped it while watching the people dance. The atmosphere was so romantic, I forgot that I didn't belong there at all. A few minutes later, a handsome young man came over to

ask me to dance, I ac-
cepted and had fun with
him. A few dances later, I
returned to my seat. A-
nother good-looking man
took an interest in me.
We danced for about
fifteen minutes. This
continued all night, I
had much
more luck with men here
than I did at singles'
bars.

Although I was having a
wonderful time, I realized
I had no place here. It
had gotten pretty late
and I had grown tired.
I checked my watch.

and it was 12:45. I de-
cided it was time to
leave. I headed back to
the window but I coul-
dn't find it. I circled the
room several times
looking for the opening.
Where was it? Eventu-
ally, I realized there were
no windows or doors. I
couldn't escape. I was
trapped.

Police still searching for young woman

Samantha Goldwin, a 22 year-old secretary has been missing for three days. Her friend, Annie O'Collins called the police after failing to contact Goldwin for two days. According to O'Collins Goldwin was acting extremely bizarre on the day of her disappearance. Kidnapping is a possibility, but she may have run away since it has become apparent that she had a psychological disorder.

About the Author

Hi! My name is Alexandra Cagen but people usually call me Sasha. This is the third book I have written. I wrote a myth book in sixth grade and last year I wrote a book about a runaway. I belong to the chorus, dance company and the independent study program. I enjoy tennis, skiing, movies, reading and shopping. In the spring, I play on a softball team.

Sasha Cagen's essays have appeared in the *San Francisco Chronicle*, *Village Voice*, and *Utne*, but she discovered her voice as a writer through zine-making (the practice of mixing one's most dearly held thoughts with images on the stapled-and-photocopied page). During the mid-'90s, she and her close friend Tara Needham co-published *Cupsize*, a revolutionary publication full of personal reflection and trenchant analysis of bisexual chic, the virtues of public vs. private education, the perils of excessive eyebrow tweezing, and more. After college graduation and a disorienting dip into the vortex of adulthood, she swapped a full-time job working in the labor movement for a part-time job proofreading to enable her to start her own magazine. Working with an all-volunteer staff in San Francisco, she launched *To-Do List*, a magazine that uses the idea of a to-do list to explore the details of daily life. *To-Do List's* premiere issue won *Utne Reader's* Alternative Press Award for Best New Magazine, Reader's Choice, 2000. She asks you to refrain from calling her "the quirkyalone" in public. Like all quirkyalones, she is so much more.

ACKNOWLEDGMENTS

Many, many quirkyalones and quirkyalone-positive people assisted in the preparation of this book. A thousand heartfelt thanks to all of you. Without your help—editorial, artistic, and emotional—the essays, lists, and brain lint that make up this book would still be lodged in various files on my computer.

THANKS TO:	FOR:
My extraordinary friends	Responding to my endless e-mail requests for suggestions for quirkyalone movies, books, deal breakers, secret single behavior, and more.
Jill Grinberg	Being the exact opposite of the stereotypical New York agent: a true human being and a powerful advocate at the same time.
Renee Sedliar	Getting quirkyalone so completely, bringing the book to HarperSanFrancisco, advocating for it in-house, and standing by its vision, in every way.
Reyhan Harmanci	Key editorial suggestions, especially in the realm of romantic obsession, and the collaboration that led to the first-ever quirkyalone-themed Mad Lib. Reyhan is my most trusted analyst of the QA condition; she has recently been named as second-in-command.
Danielle Jatlow	Oh my god. So much. Constant encouragement, editorial advice, publishing savvy, and phenomenal help securing artwork and permissions.

My father, Andrew Cagen	Reading draft after draft after draft; assuaging many neurotic fears.
Jenny Bitner	Reading draft after draft after draft; assuaging many neurotic fears.
Sara Hayden	Her friendship. Making sure that I eat when under deadline. Even though she is a self-hating quirkyalone ("Don't even try to classify me," she says), there will always be a place for Sara in the community.
Sara Cambridge	Her collaborative spirit, illustrations, and the design talent that she has brought to both quirkyalone and *To-Do List.*
Laura Beers	Her collaborative spirit and obvious design talent—we did it, we did it!
Burns Maxey	Design of www.todolistmagazine.com.
Annie Decker	The oat-cake-hockey-puck treats (and mucho help on the proposal).
Jessica Longo	Her research assistance, especially her work tracking down *Ladies' Home Journal* articles.
John Mikulenka	Expert copyediting of the proposal.
David Miller	Expert analysis of Jesus' quirkyalone status.
Ali Berzon	The Ashton Kutcher suggestion.
Roman Mars	Championing the independent press.
Tara Needham	Introducing me to Rilke.
Scott Murray	Web assistance on the *To-Do List* site.
Jodi Whitelaw	Design of the IQD-2003 site.
Shivani Ganguly, Christina Amini, Sarah Skaggs, Dano Williams, and Julie Feinstein	Editing, fact-checking, business management, and ad sales for *To-Do List.*

Kevin Kernan	Supporting my entrepreneurial spirit.
Bill Randt and Elise O'Keefe	Creating a workplace that allows people to take time off to work on their creative projects.
Marissa Walsh	Her publishing advice.
Annie Millar	All the back rubs, fact-checking support, proofreading, and more.
Chris Thomas	Always hosting me in New York.
Halo Shapiro	Listening to my woes and then taking me to the beach.
Jason Pontius	Organizing IQD-Providence-2003.
Caroline Talbot	Organizing IQD-Glasgow-2003.
Shannon O'Leary, Jeff Ray, and Liz Worthy	Organizing IQD-SF-2003.
Bethany Cagen and Erin Loura	Organizing IQD-NY-2003.
Stacy Simons	Belly dancing at IQD-SF.
Stephanie Bernstein	Singing at IQD-SF.
Andrew Boyd	Reading at IQD-NY.
Tracy Ulin	Rescuing quirkyalone from online dating profiteers. When quirkyalone.com slipped into the public domain after I neglected to renew it, Tracy bought it and gave it back to me without asking for money, no questions asked.
San Francisco	Its independent publishing community. (No other city would have provided more converts, per capita.)
My mother, Sharon	All the transcontinental love and support.
My aunt Irene	Knowing what it is like to be an artist and to struggle(!).
Denise Laws	Buying me groceries when I was too busy to shop.

Jamie Giedinghagen	Holding down the fort on the East Coast.
Alec Ramsdell	Encouraging my writing.
Dave Eggers	Early support.
Andi Zeisler	The Nancy Reaganesque red blazer.
Lisa Jervis	Paving the way in independent publishing, and being so generous with her time and advice for others who follow that path.
John McMillian	Being fun.
Carolyn Martone, Nicole Solis, Ariana Souzis, Adam Tobin, Eleni Stecopoulos, and Liz Worthy (members of my writing group)	Reading draft after draft after draft.
Danny Cagen	The mud baths.
Myself	Crossing off so many items on so many to-do lists.
All the quirkyalones everywhere	Your letters, survey responses, stories, and ideas.

> Special attention to very beginning/c
> Special attention to quiz
> Add the new ideas for the quirkyalone
> also pull in people from the Word Sea
>
> Smaller pre-MS writing tasks
> Add the spaghetti and beans SSB; al
> Add humiliating moments (final versi
> Pull in a quote from Kara Herold's ol
> into manuscript
> Add Christina Amini caption about qt
> MS
> Add Sex in the City reference to sel
> change
> headline to who wants to marry hersel
> trend that almost is
> Change that smoking pot SSB line
> Ending of chapter three
> Add the fast-forwarded relationship
> Revisit the QA nation stuff: add line
> anniversary parties and breaking up
> moving through cities like lovers; a
> about passions and hobbies to occupa
> important for quirkyalones, whether

> precise
> Think about adding a line about when quirky
> annoying. Unconventional iconoclast as a pe
> headline, or doing different exercises in a
> class.
> Think about adding Ally Sheedy from Breakf
> Quirky, or weird? Your call.
> Acknowledgments
> Chapter two and/or three: Add Reyhan in t
> womb? Also add her line about needing to
> idea.
> Add fog as an icon of the romantic
> Factcheck people?s names
> Add surfing as a passion
>
> Tabled for now
> jacket copy

CREDITS

"Quirkyalones Thoughout History: a timeline" illustration by Sara Cambridge
Emily Dickinson image from the Amherst College Archives and Special
Collections, reprinted with permission from the Trustees of Amherst College

p. 1   Photo booth photos: Christina Amini, Walt Jacobs, Shana Morris
p. 2   Frozen peas illustration by Amy Rathbone
p. 3   ATM illustration by Amy Rathbone; photo booth photo: Reyhan Harmanci
p. 4   *The Breakfast Club* photo courtesy of Universal Studios Licensing LLLP
p. 5   *Cupsize* zine by Sasha Cagen and Tara Needham
p. 6   Photo booth photo: Katie Salas; unicorn image reprinted with permission from
      Dee Dreslough; photo booth photo: Jenny Bitner; beach photo by
      Burns Maxey
p. 7   Punk vs. prep illustration by Amy Rathbone
p. 11   *People* magazine cover "Are These Old Maids?" People Weekly © 1986;
      "Will You Be a Successful Wife or an Unhappy Old Maid?" Briar Stratford, n.d.
p. 14   "The Quirkyalone: Loners are the last true romantics" courtesy of Sasha Cagen
      and *Utne* magazine
p. 15   Photo booth photo: LeVette Fuller
p. 17   "How it happened" illustration by Sara Cambridge
pp. 21–23 "Quirkyalone Nation" pie charts and text by Sara Cambridge
p. 25   Antiquirkyalone movement books illustration by Sara Cambridge
p. 26   IQD nametag by Jenny Bitner
p. 27   NY-IQD party photos by Bethany Cagen
p. 28   "Dear Self: I love you. Your consciousness" card by anonymous SF-IQD
      partygoer
p. 29   Photo collage by Laura Beers; SF-IQD party photos by Liz Worthy
p. 30   Letter reprinted with permission from Patti Sirens
p. 35   Photo booth photos: quirky friend, Linda M. Rouzan
p. 36   "Nature or nurture" chart by Sara Cambridge
p. 40   William Poy Lee photo by Christina Koci Hernandez
p. 44   Photo of Burns Maxey by Sasha Cagen
p. 45   Photo booth photo: Zarah Manos
p. 50   "Accepting or Refusing a Date" from *The Art of Dating,* Special Keepsake
      Edition, published by Association Press, New York, 1958.
p. 56   John Cusack, © 1989 Twentieth Century Fox. All rights reserved.
p. 62   Quirkyslut high heels illustration by Laura Beers
p. 64   Helen Gurley Brown © Bettman/CORBIS
p. 65   Hitachi Magic Wand illustration courtesy of Good Vibrations
pp. 66–67 Nineteenth-century vibrator ads courtesy of Good Vibrations
p. 68   Unicorn image reprinted with permission from Dee Dreslough